MATHEMATICAL CAVALCADE

Brian Bolt

CAMBRIDGE
UNIVERSITY PRESS

Published by the Press Syndicate of the University of Cambridge
The Pitt Building, Trumpington Street, Cambridge CB2 1RP
40 West 20th Street, New York, NY 10011–4211, USA
10 Stamford Road, Oakleigh, Melbourne 3166, Australia

First published 1992
Reprinted 1996

Printed in Great Britain by Scotprint Ltd, Musselburgh, Scotland

A catalogue record for this book is available from the British
Library.

Library of Congress cataloguing in publication data
Library of Congress data has been applied for.

ISBN 0 521 42617 0 paperback

Cover illustrations by Tony Hall
Text cartoons by Harry Venning

CONTENTS

Page numbers in bold refer to the puzzles;
the second page number to the commentary.

Introduction

This book has been written in response to the success of my earlier mathematical puzzle books. When half way through writing it, I was privileged to lecture to the South East Asian Conference on Mathematical Education in Brunei Darussalam, where the theme was 'The Enchantment of Mathematics'. This reinforced my experience that, given the right context, mathematics appeals to a very wide audience the world over. Mathematical recreations, whether puzzles, games or models, provide stimulating contexts. This book contains 131 such activities ranging from matchstick and coin puzzles through ferrying, railway shunting, dissection, topological and domino problems to a variety of magical number arrays with surprising properties. There are some intriguing models to make including flexagons, and a tetrahedron covered in pentominoes, while the Knight's Solitaire game is a real challenge which can amuse you for many hours.

Although a recreational book, it contains many important mathematical ideas, and the detailed commentary is essential reading *after* you have first tackled the puzzles yourself. Many of the puzzles are original, so there is something here for even the most experienced puzzler. The puzzles have not been carefully grouped together by type, but consciously mixed up to give plenty of variety for the reader, although those which are more demanding mathematically come towards the end.

I hope the book gives you as much pleasure as it gave me in compiling it.

1 One square less

(a) Change the position of, but do not remove, two matches to form exactly four squares

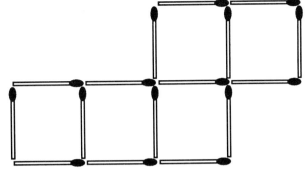

(b) Change the position of, but do not remove, three matches to form exactly three squares.

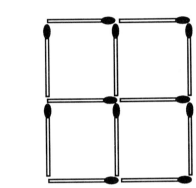

2 Only one left

Place nine coins on a 5 × 5 board as shown. A move consists of one coin jumping over another coin in an adjacent square to land in an unoccupied square on the other side of the coin being jumped over. When a coin has been jumped over it is removed. Moves can be vertical, horizontal or diagonal. The object is to end up with one coin in the centre in eight moves.

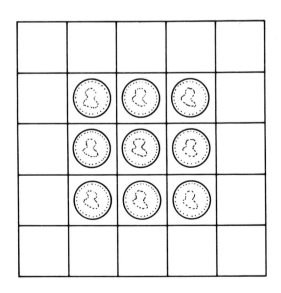

3 The eight pawns problem

Place eight pawns on a chess board so that no two pawns lie on the same row, column or diagonal.

4 Pinball pursuits

A recent sales promotion used games based on pinball tables like those shown. The challenge in each case is to find a route around the table to make as large a score as possible. The route must move from square to square either up or down, or to left or right, but not diagonally. No square can be used twice. Squares containing a black circle cannot be used. The route must end in a square on the bottom row.

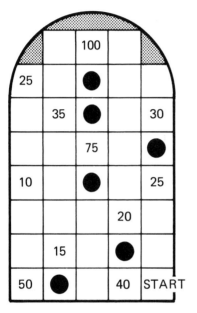

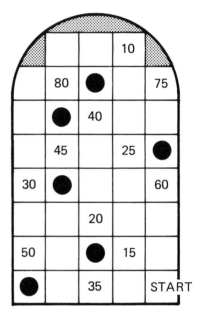

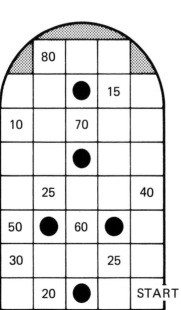

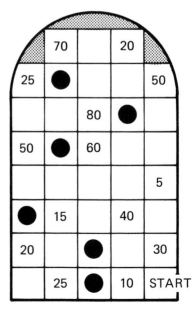

5 The tetrahedral tease

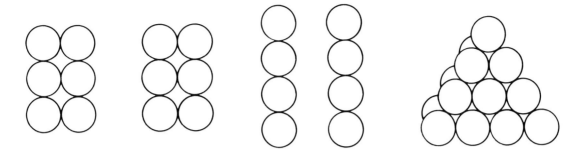

A delightful puzzle can be made from 20 wooden or polystyrene spheres as follows. Glue the spheres together to form two rectangular blocks each containing six spheres, and two strings of four spheres as shown. To make these structures robust it is a good idea to drill small holes into the spheres at their points of contact and use dowels. These can be made of matchstick or cocktail stick 'pegs' inserted into two corresponding holes of two spheres to join them together.

The puzzle is to fit the four sphere structures together to form a tetrahedron, that is a triangular-based pyramid. It may seem an impossible task at first, but patience will be rewarded!

6 Pinboard crosses

On the 5 × 5 pinboard shown, a rubber band has been placed around some of the pins to form a symmetric cross enclosing five pins and leaving four pins outside. It is also possible to make a symmetric cross enclosing five pins which leave eight pins outside. How?

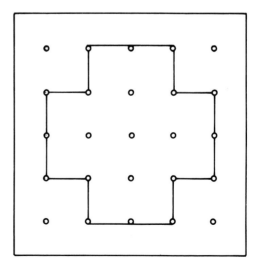

7 Be thrifty!

Each letter stands for a different number in this addition sum.

Four solutions are possible.

$$
\begin{array}{r}
\mathrm{SAVE} \\
+\mathrm{MORE} \\
\hline
\mathrm{MONEY}
\end{array}
$$

8 The apprentice's task

 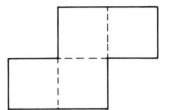

In a sheet metal shop the result of one process was to produce hundreds of shapes identical to the two above. The apprentices amused themselves in their tea breaks by seeing what shapes they could make by fitting the pieces of metal together like a jigsaw. But this got out of hand and the apprentices were forever extending their tea breaks. Their boss decided to play them at their own game, so just before going-home time on the Friday she challenged all her apprentices to make a 10 × 5 rectangle using the pieces, with the condition that no one could go home until one of them had solved the problem.

How long will it take you to solve it?

9 Catherine wheels

Put the numbers 1 to 9 into
the circles so that they total
the same along each spoke
and along each spiral. See
what solutions you can find.

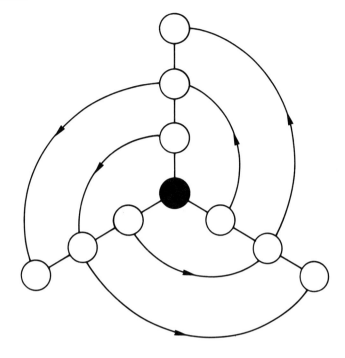

10 The intruder

A Government high-security building (see the plan) was
broken into by an intruder. The hidden security cameras
showed that, in his or her search for information, the
intruder had passed through every single doorway of the
building once only before being apprehended while trying
to open the safe.
   In which room was the safe?

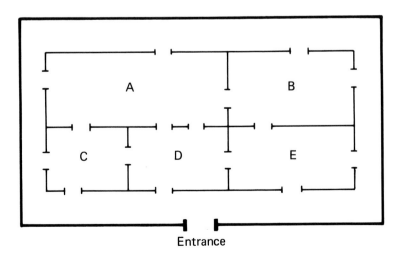

Entrance

11 An unfortunate snag

Ms Mehta had been teaching her class how to make up their own 3 × 3 magic squares. She had shown them that the magic total was always three times the number in the centre cell so that as soon as some numbers in a square are known the rest can quickly be calculated. She then gave them the square with the numbers 1 and 4 inserted as shown, and asked them to see how many different ways they could complete it using positive numbers. Lisa and Sahib each found solutions by trying out different numbers in the top left-hand cell, but Ms Mehta wasn't very happy about them for they each contained repeated numbers.

Find the pupils' solutions, and then see if you can make Ms Mehta happy!

	1	
	4	

12 Grannie Stitchwork's teddy bears

Grannie Stitchwork had a very nice sideline making teddy bears for sale in the local toyshop. Each month she made 20 identical teddys and to do this she had a delivery of: 6 m^2 of material for the fur, 5 kg of kapok for the stuffing, 4 m of coloured ribbon to tie bows around their necks, and 40 special eye buttons.

The teddys sold well, but the toyshop's market research showed that there was a steady demand for teddys of twice the size, so Grannie was asked to make 20 large ones for the following month. Always obliging, Grannie Stitchwork immediately doubled the order for all her materials for the next month.

How many large teddy bears did she make?

13 Which is the best route?

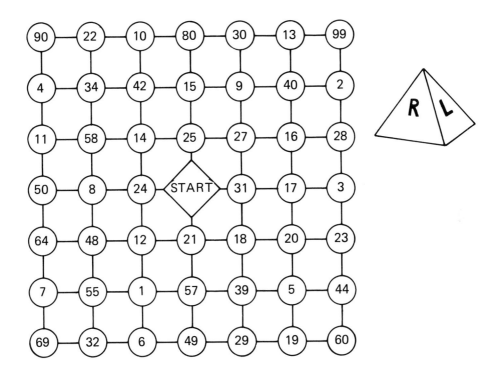

A game is played on the above board using a four-sided dice in the form of a regular tetrahedron. The faces of the dice are labelled U, D, R, L, standing for *up*, *down*, *right*, and *left*, respectively. Each player has a counter and they take turns to toss the dice. They move their counter to the adjacent circle indicated by the face of the dice which is flat against the table, unless
(a) they have already landed there, or
(b) it would move them off the board.
In this case they stay put.

Players record the numbers they land on and keep a running total. The winner is the first player to exceed 500.

The challenge is to find the smallest number of moves a player could make to win. You could easily make a board to play this game.

14 Make a folding tetrahedron

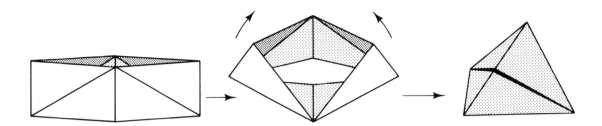

Here is a neat way of making a tetrahedron which can
fold flat in an instant. All that is required is a rectangular
piece of card 28 cm long and 4 cm wide. Divide the long
rectangle into four smaller equal rectangles and mark in
the diagonals shown.

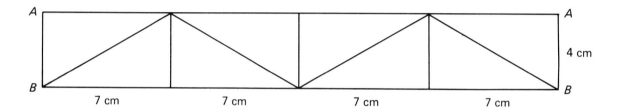

Carefully score all the vertical and diagonal lines using a
compass point or pair of scissors. Now join the ends of the
long rectangle together using sticky tape to form a band.
The band of rectangles can now be folded into the
tetrahedron. Easy to make and a very satisfying model to
handle.

15 Square the vase

You should not find it
difficult to see how to cut
the silhouette of the vase
shown in the illustration into
two identical pieces which
will fit together to make the
3 × 3 square, but can you
see how to divide it into four
identical pieces to make the
square?

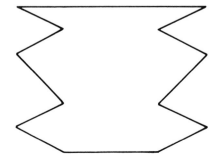

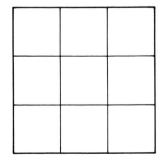

16 The newsboy's Sunday exertions

Peter lived in Spuddleton, a small country town. A map of Spuddleton's streets is shown with street lengths given in metres. To earn some pocket money Peter delivered the Sunday papers to all the streets in the town. His home is at *H* and he first has to get to the newsagent's shop at *A* to collect the papers.

How far does Peter have to walk along the streets from the time he leaves home to returning there after his paper round?

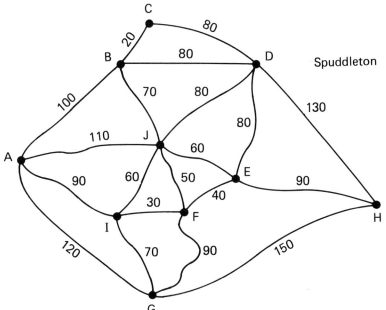

Spuddleton

17 The Josephus problem

Hegesippus tells us that, after the Romans captured Jotapat, Josephus and 40 other Jews took refuge in a cave. All but Josephus and a friend declared they would rather kill themselves than be captured. To save himself and his friend, Josephus is thought to have got everyone to agree that they would arrange themselves in a circle and that every third person be killed until one was left, who would then supposedly commit suicide! In which positions did Josephus place himself and his friend?

18 A magic domino square

Arrange the eight dominoes given to form a 4 × 4 square in such a way that the total number of spots in each row, column and diagonal is the same.

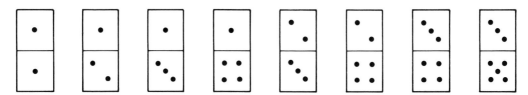

19 Triangular number patterns

The numbers 1 to 9 have been arranged in a pattern of triangles so that they total 25 along the three sides of the large triangle.

Find other arrangements of the numbers to make the totals equal.

What are the largest and smallest totals obtainable?

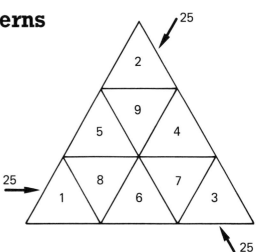

20 A two touching transformation

Arrange eight coins to form the H pattern shown. By moving one coin at a time, by sliding it into a position where it *touches two other coins*, form the square pattern shown. It can be achieved in four moves.

Now try to transform the square back to the H pattern. This is not as easy as it appears for you cannot simply reverse the moves you used to solve the first puzzle. How many moves did you need?

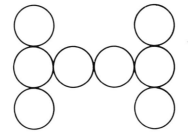
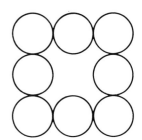

21 Knight's Solitaire

This is an interesting version of solitaire. It consists of a 5 × 5 board and two sets of twelve pieces, arranged as shown with the middle square vacant. The challenge is to interchange the two sets of pieces in as few moves as possible. A move is the same as a knight's move in the game of chess – to move a piece to the square which has been left vacant by the previous move.

One commercial version of the game says, '50 to 55 moves is average, less than 50 is good, less than 45 is excellent'. Which are you?

You could make your own version of the game using coloured counters or coins.

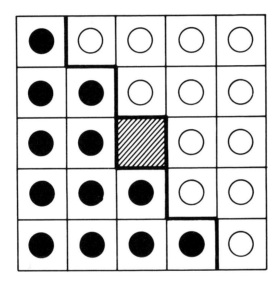

22 Matchstick magic

This hexagonal wheel of six equilateral triangles is made from twelve matches. By moving just four matches the wheel can be turned into a figure consisting of three equilateral triangles. How?

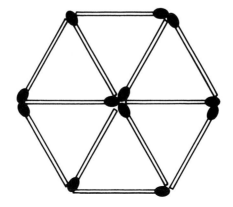

23 Coaxial contortions

A householder wants to connect the existing television aerial at *A* by expensive coaxial cable to a point *B* in the wall of a new extension as shown in the diagram. *B* is centrally placed and 1 m below the flat roof.

What is the shortest cable required to join *A* to *B* if it is always to remain in contact with the surfaces of the building? Where does the cable leave the sloping roof?

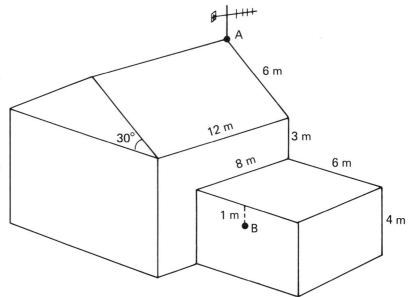

24 Double up!

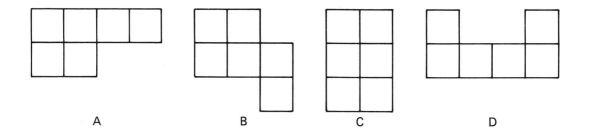

A   B   C   D

The four shapes above are known as hexominoes because they each consist of six squares. What is fascinating about this set is that the four pieces can all be fitted together, like a jigsaw, to make double-sized versions of each of them. Cut out a set of these shapes and form their enlargements. How long did it take you?

25 Generating magic squares using the NE rule

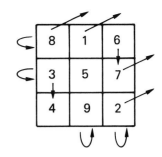

The figure shows 3 × 3 and 5 × 5 magic squares which have been obtained by the NE rule. This rule is a method of filling in magic squares, of odd order, by starting in the middle of the top edge, and moving diagonally to the right and up, counting as you go. When at any edge of the square you must imagine it rolled into a tube so that its opposite edges are joined together. Then, for example, 24 at the top edge is followed by 25 at the bottom edge, one column to the right. Similarly, 22 at the right-hand edge is followed by 23 on the left-hand edge, one row higher up.

Sometimes a cell on the diagonal path being followed has already been used, then the rule is to drop down one cell and continue on the lower diagonal. A good example of this can be seen by following the sequence 18, 19, 20, 21, 22.

Study the paths followed in the examples given, and then use the same method to generate magic squares of orders 7 × 7 and 9 × 9.

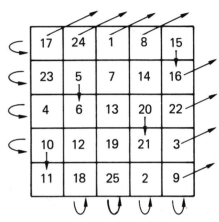

What is fascinating is an adaptation of this method using a knight's move at each stage. The 5 × 5 square shown here was produced by always trying to move two cells to the right and one up. Some extra cells have been added to the edge of the square to show how the route was constructed. The result is quite different from the 5 × 5 square above, although they necessarily have the same magic total, 65.

What would happen if you used a different basic step such as three right and two up? See what you can discover.

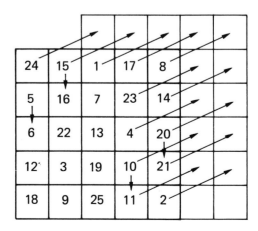

26 Wedding preparations

Farmer Giles' three daughters Louise, Nancy and Susannah had fed well on butter and clotted cream, so when a date was set for Nancy's wedding, they made a pact with each other to lose weight. To aid them in their slimming campaign they decided to weigh themselves regularly, but the only scales available to them were a set used for weighing cattle, which started at 100 kg. Now, heavy as they were, not one of them exceeded 100 kg. Susannah was not to be defeated, however, as she had most weight to lose. She reckoned that by weighing themselves in pairs it would be possible to deduce their individual weights. At the start of their slim:

Louise and Nancy together weighed 132 kg
Nancy and Susannah together weighed 151 kg
Susannah and Louise together weighed 137 kg

What did they each weigh?
It is not recorded what they weighed on Nancy's wedding day!

27 Olive Orchard's cider measures

Olive Orchard's cider was renowned for its flavour and potency throughout the region and she had a steady stream of customers to her door. She was also notorious for her eccentric way of measuring out the cider for her customers. She had just two measures which she had inherited from her grandfather, one with a capacity of 4 litres, and one of 7 litres. Using these she was very skilled at measuring out any number of litres a customer ordered.

How would you use the measures to satisfy a customer who asked for 2 litres? No cider is to be wasted but you can, if you wish, pour some back into the barrel.

14

28 Star puzzle 1

Fill in the star with the numbers 1, 2, 3, . . . , 12, one number to each triangle, so that the totals of the four numbers, in a row from point to opposite point, are all the same.

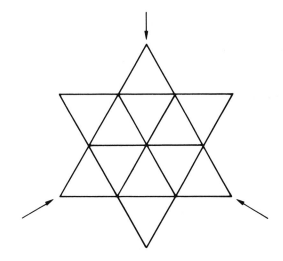

29 Domino products

The four dominoes shown have been arranged to form a hollow square in such a way that the product of the numbers of spots along each side of the square is 12.

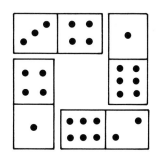

Select dominoes from the eight given below to form similar squares where the product is (a) 18, (b) 30, (c) 36.

30 When was Jane born?

When David is twice as old as he is now he will be four times as old as his daughter Jane will be in five years time. If in 1990, four years ago, he was four times as old as his daughter, in what year was she born?

15

31 A tetrahedron from pentominoes

This is a fascinating model to make, for when finished you will have a tetrahedron whose faces are made up of all twelve pentominoes. If the pentominoes are coloured individually the model will be particularly attractive.

Start by drawing a 12 × 5 rectangle, preferably on thin card, and then draw in the twelve pentominoes as shown, or use any other arrangement you know. Now draw in the diagonal lines to form the triangles which when folded will be the faces of the tetrahedron. Score the diagonal lines to aid folding, and add tabs for sticking the model together.

As shown, face ACD of the final tetrahedron will be produced from the two triangles APC and $A'P'D$. Experienced model makers will probably prefer that triangle APC is drawn as an extension of triangle $A'P'D$ so that face ACD does not have a join down the middle.

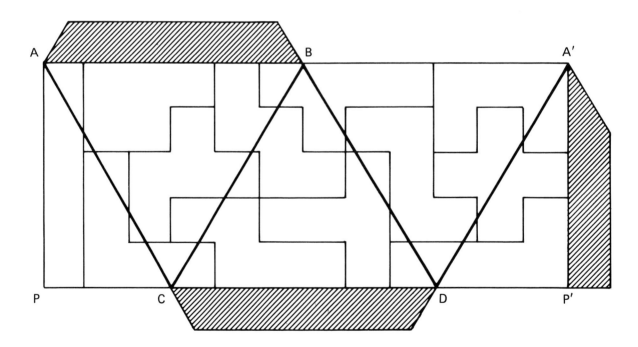

32 Formation dancing

Three male and three female ballroom dancers are in a line as shown, and the choreographer wants to devise different ways to change to an alternating female/male pattern.

What is the smallest number of moves required if this is to be achieved by

(a) adjacent pairs of dancers changing places, or

(b) a pair of adjacent dancers moving together, in the same order, to the end of the line or a suitable space in the line?

33 The gardener's predicament

Lady Floribunda was very proud of her rose garden, not just for the large variety of roses it contained, but for the clever ways in which she arranged them. One day she presented her gardener with four white roses and three red roses, with the instruction to plant them in such a way that they would form six lines of three rose bushes, with two white bushes and one red bush in each row. She knew it was possible, for she had seen the design in a specialist rose growers' magazine, but of course she couldn't find it now.

The gardener was baffled! Can you help out?

34 Fair shares for all

A square building site is represented by sixteen matches. The small square inside represents a pond which the builder wishes to retain. Planning permission has been given to build five houses and the builder wishes to divide the site, so that, apart from the pond, each house has a plot of land of an identical shape and size.

Show how this can be done by the addition of ten matches.

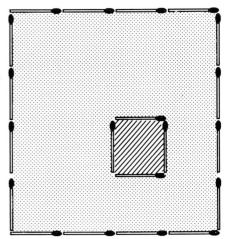

35 Count the trains

On the London Underground, Circle line trains leave Paddington on the hour and at 10-minute intervals in both directions, clockwise and anticlockwise. Each train takes $1\frac{1}{2}$ hours to complete the circuit and return to Paddington. If you make a journey in one of the trains from Paddington, and travel clockwise, how many trains would you meet coming in the opposite direction before you next arrive at Paddington?

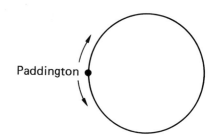

36 Isoperimetric shapes

The two shapes shown are made from six identical square tiles which are so arranged that their perimeters are each 12 units, where a unit of length corresponds to the length of the edge of a tile. Investigate all the possible shapes with a perimeter of 12 units which can be made using all the six tiles.

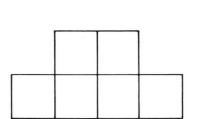

37 Number patterns

There are many fascinating number patterns. Here are two to investigate. Complete the following:

(a)
$$8 \times 8 + 13 =$$
$$88 \times 8 + 13 =$$
$$888 \times 8 + 13 =$$
$$8888 \times 8 + 13 =$$
$$88888 \times 8 + 13 =$$

(b)
$$1 \times 1 \quad =$$
$$11 \times 11 \quad =$$
$$111 \times 111 \quad =$$
$$1111 \times 1111 \quad =$$
$$11111 \times 11111 \quad =$$

Do these patterns extend indefinitely?

38 Navigational hazards

A group of three explorers had travelled for many weeks through the tropical rain forest with three native guides. Their equipment included a light inflatable dinghy which they used to cross the many rivers they encountered. However, the dinghy could only take two people at a time, and only one of the explorers and one of the natives could successfully operate it. Further, the explorers learned that the natives were from a tribe of head hunters, so they were not willing to be outnumbered on any river bank by them. In spite of this they had worked out a way of safely negotiating all the rivers.

   What is the smallest number of crossings needed to get the party across a river?

39 Square the goblet

Show how to divide the goblet shown into four identical pieces which can be rearranged to form a square. It helps to know that the outline of the goblet is formed from quadrants of identical circles.

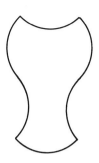

40 Reptiles!

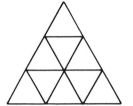

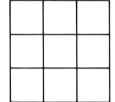

Triangular tiles and square tiles can be fitted together to cover larger areas of the same shape, as shown above. But many other shapes of tile have this same replicating property. Below are three examples.

First cut out four of each of the shapes shown from card or paper and fit them together to make similar shapes of twice their original size.

Now comes the real challenge. Use nine of each shape and fit them together to make similar shapes of three times their original size.

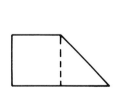
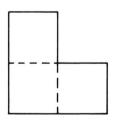
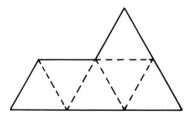

41 Turn Summer into Spring

These two summer months add up to give a month in spring if you choose numbers carefully to substitute for each of the letters.

$$
\begin{array}{r}
\text{JUNE} \\
+\text{JULY} \\
\hline
\text{APRIL}
\end{array}
$$

42 Four in a line

Twelve coins can be placed on the table so that eight straight lines can be drawn, each of which passes through the centres of four of the coins. How?

43 The ring main

An electrician has to put in a cable to connect the twelve power sockets shown in a single loop. What route should be taken to minimise the length of cable required?

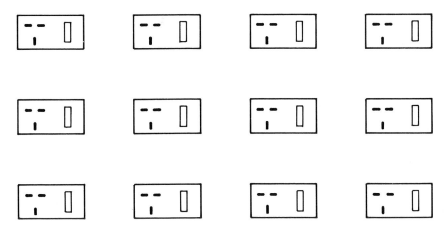

44 This looks easy!

What is the largest number of regions this ring could be divided into using three straight lines?

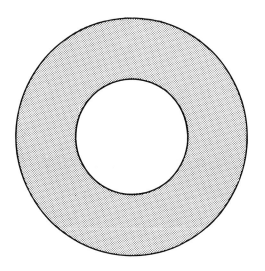

45 Have fun with a flexagon tube

Flexagons consist of bands of polygons linked together in ways which allow them to be 'flexed' into a wide variety of shapes along the edges of the polygons. They were originally discovered in 1939 by Arthur Stone, a young English mathematician.

One of the simplest to make is shown here. Cut out a rectangle from thin card equivalent to four squares (20 cm × 5 cm is an appropriate size) and draw in the diagonals of the squares. Carefully score all the lines and flex the rectangle along each of them to ensure ease of movement. Colour the two sides of the rectangle in distinctive colours, and then join its ends to form a tube-like cube without a top or bottom. Now by a series of folds, using the edges and diagonals of the squares, it is possible to turn the tube inside out. On the way you will find all kinds of intriguing configurations, including a tube of approximately half the height of the original.

If at first you don't succeed, try, try again!

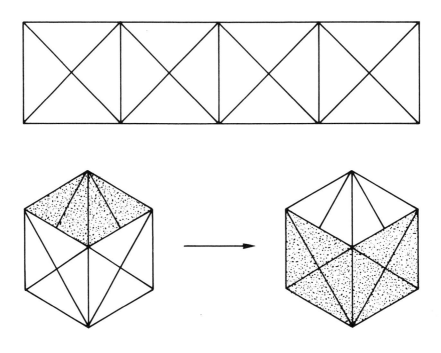

46 The giant and the dwarfs

This is a game for two players. The board shown here can easily be drawn on a piece of paper, but a more permanent version could be made by drilling holes in a block of wood and using coloured pegs for pieces, or making hollow depressions for the circles and using marbles as pieces.

Three counters are required for the three dwarfs (D) and a counter of a different colour or size is required for the giant (G). The starting position is shown. One of the dwarfs moves first and they can move down or across to any adjacent cell which is not already occupied. Thus for example in the opening move the left-hand dwarf could move straight down to circle 2, or diagonally to circle 1. The giant can move in a similar way but it is also allowed to move up the board.

The object of the game is for the dwarfs to surround the giant so that it cannot move.

Play the game and see if you can devise a winning strategy.

What would happen if you tried a different starting position for the pieces?

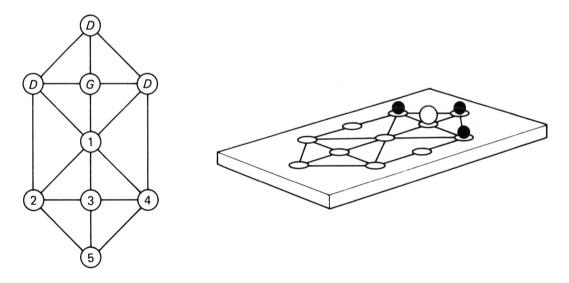

47 Surprise, surprise!

Take any 3-digit number and use your calculator to multiply it by 13. Now multiply the product by 7, and the new product formed by 11. What do you find? Can you explain your findings?

48 A kind of magic

Choose any number from the array, say 39. Now choose a second number not in the same row or column as the first, say 24. Next choose a third number in a different row or column from those already chosen, say 10. Choose a fourth number, again in a different row or column from those already chosen, say 8. This leaves only one number, 3, in a row or column not already used. The five numbers chosen add up to 84. Now the fascinating property of this array of numbers is that, no matter how you make your five choices, following the same rules, their total will always be 84.

Try it for yourself then try to explain why it works!

13	9	22	(8)	18
24	20	33	19	29
5	1	14	0	(10)
30	26	(39)	25	35
7	(3)	16	2	12

49 How old was the Rev. Pascal?

The Rev. Pascal married quite late in life to one of his admiring parishioners who was many years younger than him. As an amateur dabbler in number relationships he reckoned that he would be ready to retire when his wife was as old as he had been on their wedding day. Further, at his retirement, on the anniversary of their wedding, the sum of all his ages, in years from his wedding day to his retirement would total 1000.

What were the ages of the Rev. Pascal and his wife on their wedding day?

50 Envelopes of curves

'To envelope', the dictionary tells us, is 'to wrap up' or 'to surround'. We use an envelope to put a letter or card in before sending it through the post, and mathematicians use the word when they have a family of lines (or other curves) which surround a shape. In the drawing the lines seem to form a circle, although the circle itself is not drawn, and are said to be an envelope.

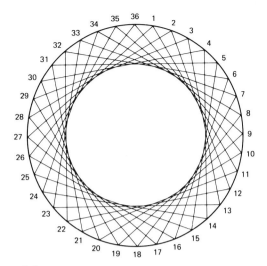

To draw this envelope and others in this activity you will first need to draw a large circle (say 10 cm diameter) and mark off 36 points on the circumference. This is easy with a protractor, for the points will be at 10° intervals when measured from the centre of the circle.

The envelope of the circle shown above is then achieved by joining every point labelled n by a straight line to the point labelled $n + 10$. When $n + 10$ exceeds 36 just subtract 36 to find the correct point. For example, when $n = 29$, then $n + 10 = 39$ so take away 36 to leave 3.

Investigate the envelope obtained when straight lines are drawn from n to $n + 5$, n to $n + 15$, n to $n + 25$ etc.

More intriguing envelopes are obtained by using other rules to join the points.

The cardioid, meaning heart-shaped, is formed by joining 1 to 2, 2 to 4, 3 to 6, 4 to 8, 5 to 10, . . . , n to $2n$.

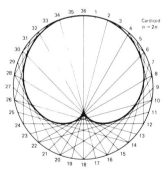

The nephroid, meaning kidney-shaped, is formed by joining 1 to 3, 2 to 6, 3 to 9, 4 to 12, 5 to 15, . . . , n to $3n$.

Investigate the effect of using other rules.

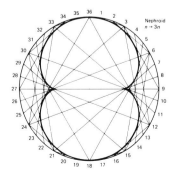

51   The biker's challenge

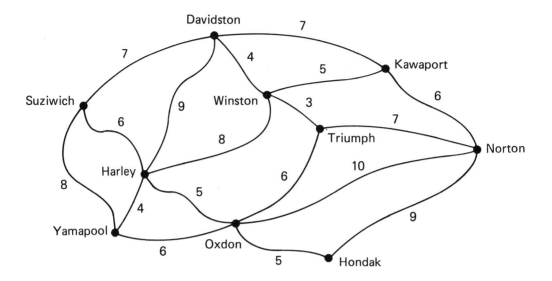

A motorcycle club organised a bank-holiday competition. The bikers assembled at Suziwich, where they were given the above map and challenged to find the shortest route which would take them along all the roads shown, at least once, and end up at their favourite restaurant. The numbers on the map represent the distances between towns in miles.

What is the shortest distance anyone could travel to satisfy the conditions, and where is the biker's favourite restaurant?

52   Count the spots

A set of dominoes consists of rectangular tiles each carrying two numbers from 0, 1, 2, 3, 4, 5, 6 represented by patterns of spots. Every possible pairing of numbers occurs just once, including each number with itself.

How many dominoes are there in a set? How many spots are there on a set of dominoes?

53 Magic windmills

Fit the numbers 1 to 8 into the squares so that the totals along each of the four sails of the windmill are equal.

How many solutions can you find?

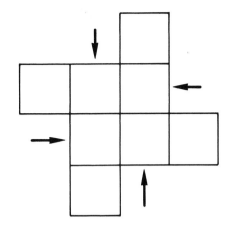

54 Only six straight lines

It is easy to draw seven straight lines that connect all sixteen dots in the 4 × 4 array without taking your pencil off the paper, but it can be done using only six straight lines. Can you do it?

55 Correct these sums

These two sums can be corrected by choosing suitable digits to substitute for the letters.

(a)
```
      TWO
    x TWO
    ─────
    THREE
```

(b)
```
     THREE
   + THREE
      FOUR
   ───────
    ELEVEN
```

56 Railway rotations

A city rail network is as shown with nine stations represented by the squares. The city has eight trains numbered *A* to *H* and they end the day at the stations shown. Ideally the traffic controller would like to start the next day with the trains in alphabetical order, one in each of the stations on the outer ring. How can he achieve this with as few train movements as possible if each train movement must end at an empty station?

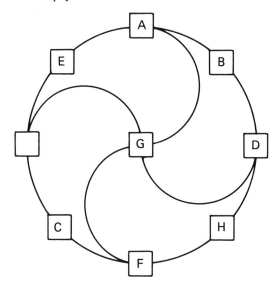

57 Back in line!

Arrange sixteen coins in a square array so that the coins alternate heads and tails (or use black and white pawns from a chess set). Your task is to rearrange the coins so that in each column the coins are either all heads, or all tails. But in order to do this you are only allowed to touch *two* coins.

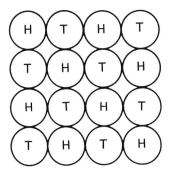

28

58 Remove a rectangle

This is a game for two players. Start with a rectangular array of dots, for example a 5×7 array as shown.

A move consists of selecting a point in the array such as A and removing from the field of play all the points in the rectangle to the left and below the point.

Players take turns to play and the loser is the person forced to select the last dot, which of course will always be at the top right-hand corner.

A typical game is shown below where A plays first and chooses points $A_1, A_2, \ldots$ while B chooses $B_1, B_2, \ldots$ and forces A to play the losing move.

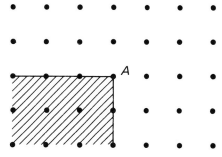

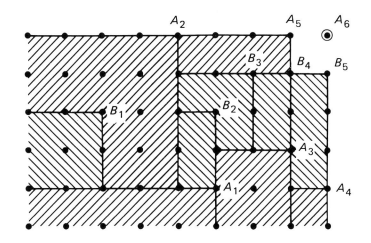

Can you develop a winning strategy?

59 Measuring the diagonal of a brick

How can you use a ruler to measure the length of the long diagonal from one corner of a brick to its opposite corner?

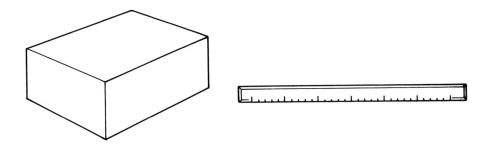

60 Domino knots

Many interesting designs can be made using all 28
dominoes from a standard double-six set, such as the two
knot designs shown here. They can be made in such a way
that, where two dominoes meet, the number of spots on
the dominoes match. Many solutions are possible, but can
you find one?

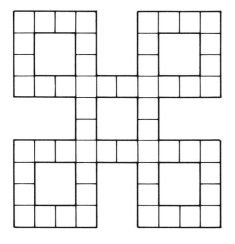
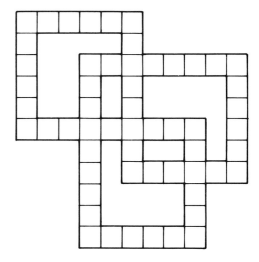

61 Jinxed!

Leela enjoyed living in a large city, but one of the
drawbacks was having to live in a 20-storey skyscraper
with only one available lift shaft. She was convinced that
the lift had a jinx on her, for it seemed that whenever she
wanted the lift to go down to work, it was four times as
likely to be going up as coming down. You must
appreciate that this was a very unsophisticated lift which
once having started on an upward journey, had to travel
to the top of the building before descending all the way
down again.

How can you explain Leela's observations?

62 Make yourself a hexaflexagon

A hexaflexagon is an intriguing arrangement of equilateral triangles folded in such a way that at any time six of them form a hexagon. The flexagon can be 'flexed' into a new arrangement by pinching together two adjacent triangles and opening out the triangles from the centre to reveal a new face. When you have made a flexagon mark the corners of the triangles at the centre of the visible hexagon with a symbol such as a heart or diamond, or spell out a six-letter word. Then flex the hexaflexagon and mark the centre of the new face with another set of symbols. You will be surprised just how many different centres you can find! With a lot of patience you could stick parts of a picture like a jigsaw to the centre cut from a christmas card for example.

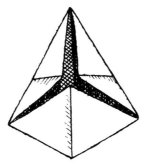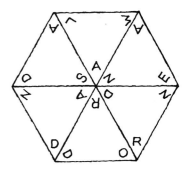

Now for the method of construction.

(a)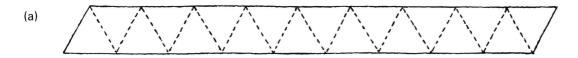

On a strip of thin card draw eighteen equilateral triangles as in (a). You will find 5 cm a good size for the side of a triangle.

Score along each of the dotted sides of the triangles. On one side number the triangles 1, 2, 3, 1, 2, 3, . . . , and mark the end triangles along the edge as in (b).

(b)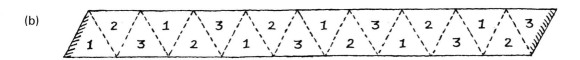

Turn the strip over and number the other side with a 4,
4, 5, 5, 6, 6, . . . pattern exactly like diagram (c).

(c)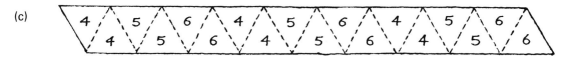

Next fold the strip by placing triangle 4 onto triangle 4,
5 onto 5, 6 onto 6 etc., as in (d). This rolls the strip up
(see (e)).

(d)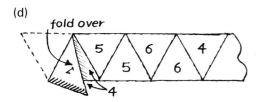

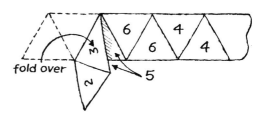

(e)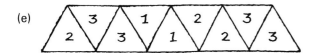

Now fold the strip again so that triangles of the same
number are all on top, as shown in (f).

(f)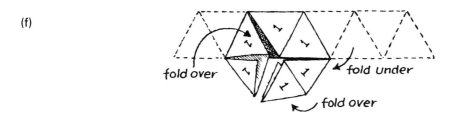

Stick the two marked edges together using sellotape.

63 The diabolical cyclone

The numbers 1 to 16 have been put into the diamonds in the wheel shown so that all the totals on each spoke, and on each circle come to 34. There are hundreds of ways in which this may be achieved, but the challenge is to find one where the numbers on all the spirals, like the two shown dotted, also total 34.

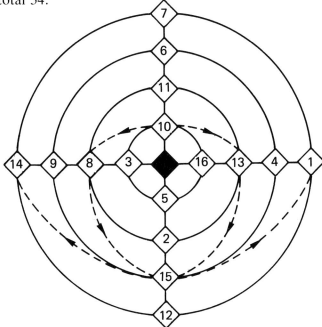

64 Two coin conundrums

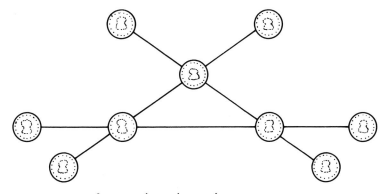

The drawing shows one way of arranging nine coins so that there are three lines with four coins in each line.

1 Find a way of arranging twelve coins to form six lines with four coins in each.
2 Now the real challenge is for you to arrange ten coins in such a way that they form six lines with four coins in each.

65 Triangular stamps

In order to boost its economy, a small tropical island published an attractive set of stamps in the shape of equilateral triangles. These were sold in groups of four, as shown, with denominations *a*, *b*, *c* and *d* in such a way that the purchaser could tear off a stamp, or connected block of stamps, to the value of 1 cent, 2 cents, 3 cents, . . . , 10 cents. How was this achieved? Could you do better?

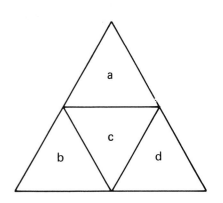

66 Decimated!

It was the weekly games period for the fifth year, which contained fifteen boys and fifteen girls. The games teacher wanted to divide them into two teams in as fair a way as possible, so she asked them to form a circle. Then, starting at one of the boys, she counted clockwise choosing every tenth person until she had one team of fifteen. The remaining fifteen pupils would then form the other team. Imagine her surprise when she ended up with a team of all boys and a team of all girls. The last thing she wanted!

In what order were the boys and girls arranged around the circle?

Would the games teacher have had more success if she had counted in sevens instead of tens?

67 The vanishing act

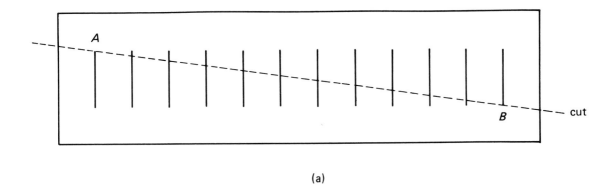

(a)

On a sheet of paper carefully draw twelve lines each 3 cm
long and 2 cm apart as shown. Then carefully cut the
paper into two along the line AB which joins the top of
the first line to the bottom of the last line.

   Now slide the two pieces of paper along the cut edge
until the lines first coincide as in diagram (b).

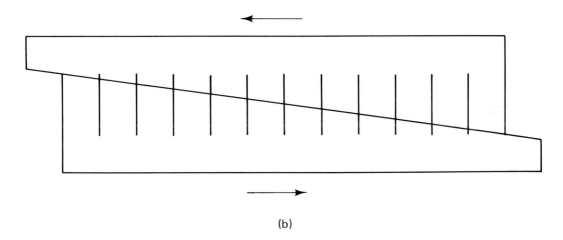

(b)

   How many lines are there now? How can you account
for the apparent discrepancy?

68 Locate the primes

There are 362 880 different possible nine-digit numbers
which can be formed using each of the digits 1, 2, 3, . . . ,
9 only once. How many of these numbers are prime?

69 WARTS into STRAW!

Place five identical cubes in a line on squared paper.
Carefully draw the letters W A R T S onto the top faces
as shown. (Children's bricks or sugar cubes could be
used.) You are now permitted to roll a cube about one of
its edges through 90° onto an adjacent square as long as it
is not occupied. The challenge is to transform the word
WARTS into the word STRAW on the same five squares
by suitably rolling the cubes. The smaller the number of
rolls the better!

70 All present!

Generating numbers which contain all the digits 1, 2,
3, . . . , 9 has a fascination all of its own. Unfortunately,
many calculators only display eight digits, so some
ingenuity will be needed. The squares of the following
numbers all produce numbers of this kind:

$$11\ 826^2 = \qquad 19\ 377^2 =$$
$$12\ 543^2 = \qquad 19\ 629^2 =$$
$$15\ 681^2 = \qquad 23\ 178^2 =$$
$$18\ 072^2 = \qquad 29\ 034^2 =$$

There are in fact 75 further square numbers of this type.
How many can you find?

71 Catch your shadow

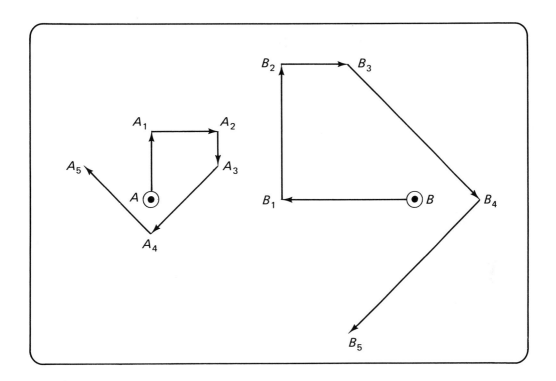

Starting at A a person can trace out a route on the visual display unit of a computer. The computer has been programmed to start at B and produce an image of A's trace having transformed it in a systematic way. The challenge is for the person operating the computer to decide what transformation is taking place and then to construct a route so that A and B coincide. One person's attempt is shown on the screen above and should be more than sufficient for you to see what transformation is taking place, but can you catch your shadow?

72 Prime magic

This magic square has the special property that all its entries are prime numbers. There are ten such magic squares where no number exceeds 300, but content yourself with finding the only one whose magic total is less than the one shown here.

103	79	37
7	73	139
109	67	43

73 Amoeboid patterns

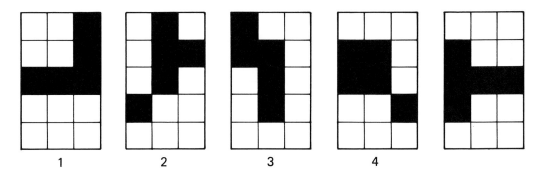

1   2   3   4

Amoebas move by changing their shape. This amoeba has
a constant area of five squares and lives in a 3 × 5
rectangular tank! It changes its shape in a very systematic
way as illustrated by the above sequence. Identify the
rule(s) which govern the change in the amoeba's shape
and investigate the ensuing shapes in the sequence. Will it
ever return to the first shape above?

74 Waste not, want not!

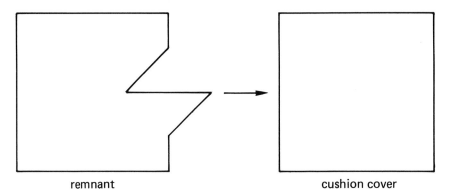

remnant   cushion cover

Mrs Patchwork regularly visited her local remnant shop to
look for bargains. One day she saw a beautiful piece of
material which she thought would make a cushion cover,
but on closer inspection she was disappointed to see it had
a jagged edge. However, she was a great improviser and
soon realised how she could cut the material into four
identical pieces which could be sewn together, without any
waste, to make a square cover for her cushion. Indeed she
felt the symmetrical pattern formed by the four pieces
enhanced her cover. How did she do it?

75 Multigrades

Sets of numbers can be found with the fascinating property that, not only are their sums equal, but also the sums of their squares, and the sums of their cubes, and even higher powers are equal. For example:

$$1 + 8 + 7 + 14 = 2 + 4 + 11 + 13$$
$$1^2 + 8^2 + 7^2 + 14^2 = 2^2 + 4^2 + 11^2 + 13^2$$
$$1^3 + 8^3 + 7^3 + 14^3 = 2^3 + 4^3 + 11^3 + 13^3$$

This is known as a third-order multigrade. But how can you find such sets for yourself?

Start with a simple equality such as

$$1 + 5 = 2 + 4$$

Add k to each term to get

$$(1 + k) + (5 + k) = (2 + k) + (4 + k)$$

then swop sides and add to the first equality to give

$$1 + 5 + (2 + k) + (4 + k) = 2 + 4 + (1 + k) + (5 + k)$$

you will now find that

$$1^2 + 5^2 + (2 + k)^2 + (4 + k)^2 = 2^2 + 4^2 + (1 + k)^2 + (5 + k)^2$$

is also true for any value of k, so we have a second-order multigrade. When $k = 5$, for example,

$$1 + 5 + 7 + 9 = 2 + 4 + 6 + 10$$
$$1^2 + 5^2 + 7^2 + 9^2 = 2^2 + 4^2 + 6^2 + 10^2$$

When $k = 4$, $1 + k = 5$ and as this number occurs on both sides of the equality it can be left out, leaving

$$1 + 6 + 8 = 2 + 4 + 9$$
$$1^2 + 6^2 + 8^2 = 2^2 + 4^2 + 9^2$$

To form a third-order multigrade use the same process as before, but start with a second-order multigrade. Adding 5 to each of the numbers in the above example, swopping sides, and then adding to the original equality gives

$$1 + 6 + 8 + 7 + 9 + 14 = 2 + 4 + 9 + 6 + 11 + 13$$

and leaving out the numbers common to both sides we have the third-order multigrade

$$1^n + 7^n + 8^n + 14^n = 2^n + 4^n + 11^n + 13^n$$

for $n = 1, 2, 3$

Use the same process with this set as a starting point to form a fourth-order multigrade, and so on for higher orders.

76 Calculator golf

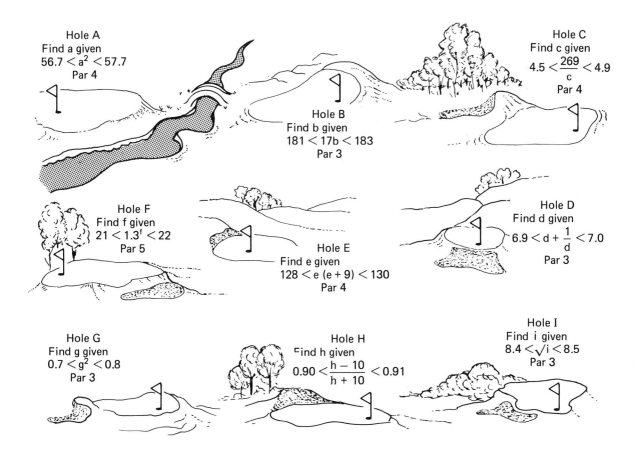

Hole A
Find a given
$56.7 < a^2 < 57.7$
Par 4

Hole B
Find b given
$181 < 17b < 183$
Par 3

Hole C
Find c given
$4.5 < \dfrac{269}{c} < 4.9$
Par 4

Hole F
Find f given
$21 < 1.3^f < 22$
Par 5

Hole E
Find e given
$128 < e\,(e + 9) < 130$
Par 4

Hole D
Find d given
$6.9 < d + \dfrac{1}{d} < 7.0$
Par 3

Hole G
Find g given
$0.7 < g^2 < 0.8$
Par 3

Hole H
Find h given
$0.90 < \dfrac{h - 10}{h + 10} < 0.91$

Hole I
Find i given
$8.4 < \sqrt{i} < 8.5$
Par 3

This is a game based on your ability to estimate. You will
need a calculator and a means of recording your
estimates. To play a hole, make an estimate of a number
for the letter and use your calculator to work out the
value of the calculation indicated. If this number lies
between the limits indicated you will have 'holed in one'.
This is unlikely, so record your estimate and the result of
the calculation. From this you should be in a position to
make a better estimate and get nearer to the hole.

Make further estimates and test their accuracy with your
calculator until your estimate lands you in the hole
between the limits. The number of estimates you require
for a hole is your score.

Above is a nine-hole course with suggested pars for
each hole. The par is the estimated standard score for the
hole that a good player should make. Can you match par
or better? Make up a similar course yourself and challenge
your friends.

77 The starting grid

In a saloon car race there were five teams, A, B, C, D
and E, each with five cars labelled 1, 2, 3, 4 and 5
respectively. The starting grid had five rows and the cars
were five abreast in a 5 × 5 array. To make the start as
fair as possible it was arranged that in any row, or
column, or diagonal of the starting grid, there would be
only one car from each team, and only one car with each
number.

Find a possible starting arrangement for the cars.

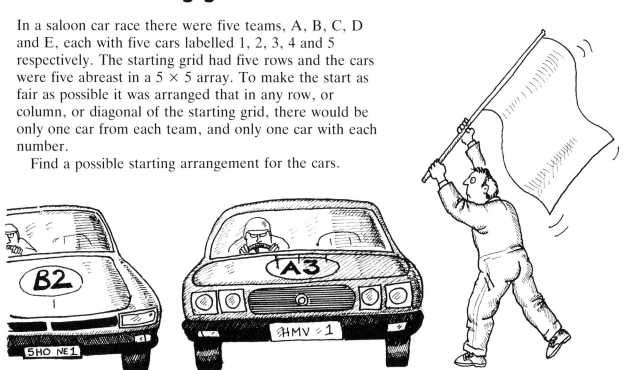

78 Intersecting circles

No matter how you draw two intersecting circles on a
piece of paper or on the surface of a sphere the effect is
to divide the surface into four distinct regions.

There is at least one surface, however, on which you
can draw two intersecting circles, leaving the surface as
one interconnected region. Explain!

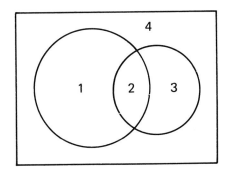

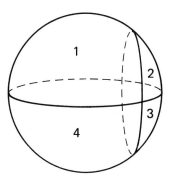

79 Can you help the block manufacturer?

A manufacturer was keen to design a new size of concrete block with the property that if it was cut in half through the plane of symmetry which bisected its long edges then the resulting halves would have exactly the same shape as the original block.

He wanted the shortest edge of the block to be 10 cm. What lengths should he make the other edges?

80 The cyclo-cross race

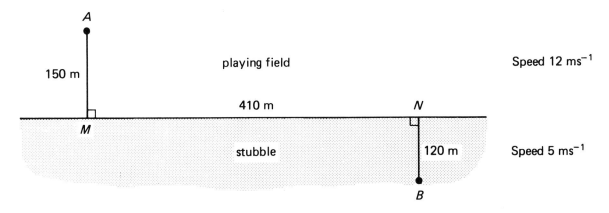

In a cyclo-cross race the cyclists enter a playing field at A. They have to cross this before crossing the stubble of a recently harvested cornfield and leaving it at a gate B. The boundary between the playing field and the cornfield is a straight line which can be crossed by the cyclists where they please. Now the cyclists hope to average 12 ms^{-1} across the playing field but only 5 ms^{-1} across the stubble. See the diagram.

Where would you suggest the cyclists cross the boundary MN and how quickly should they be able to cycle from A to B?

42

81 The unusual jigsaw

Professor Dissection's daughter Irene loved doing jigsaws and became quite an expert at quickly completing puzzles with up to 3000 pieces. To give her a new challenge the professor designed a jigsaw with only nine pieces. But all the pieces were square, no two pieces were the same size, and they were all painted red (Irene's favourite colour), so no help to fitting the pieces together. All Irene had to do was to fit them together to form a rectangle. The sides of the squares were of length:

   1 cm, 4 cm, 7 cm, 8 cm, 9 cm, 10 cm, 14 cm, 15 cm, 18 cm
   Can you complete the jigsaw?

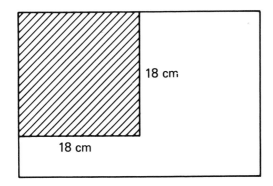

82 Palindromic termini

38 added to 83 gives 121 which is palindromic as the digits read the same from left to right as from right to left. What other two-digit numbers have this property?

   Starting with 68 and adding 86 gives 154 which is not palindromic, but if the process is repeated by reversing the digits of the sum and adding it to itself the result will eventually be palindromic:

   68 + 86 = 154   not palindromic
   154 + 451 = 605   not palindromic
   605 + 506 = 1111   palindromic

The number of steps required may be small or large: 89 for example, requires 24 steps before the sum becomes palindromic. No one has yet determined whether this will happen when 196 is taken as the starting point.

   Investigate what happens when starting with other numbers – you need not restrict yourself to two-digit numbers as a starting point.

83 Star puzzle 2

The numbers 1, 3, 5, 7, 9, 11, 10, 12, 13, 14, 15, 17, have been arranged in the six-pointed star so that the totals of the five numbers along each of the six lines indicated are all equal to 45. Magic!

The challenge for you is to create a similar magic star using the numbers 1, 2, 3, 4, . . . , 12. There are only two solutions.

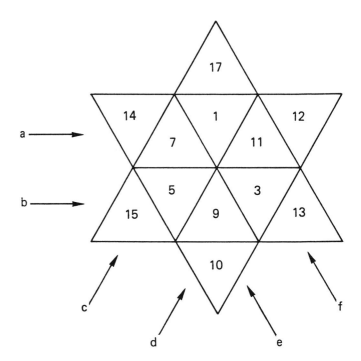

84 About turn!

Three-digit numbers exist so that

$$abc \times def = ghijk \quad \text{and} \quad cba \times fed = kjihg$$

are both true at the same time, such as

$$131 \times 111 = 14541 \quad \text{and} \quad 102 \times 201 = 20502$$

But these rely on a degree of symmetry to work. What is remarkable, however, is that such numbers exist which exhibit no symmetry. Can you find any of them?

85 Quadrilles

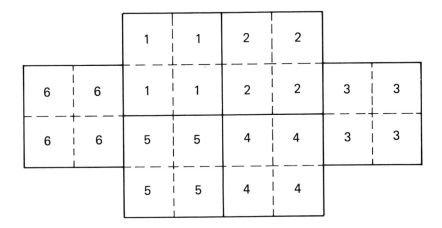

Select the appropriate twelve dominoes from a standard double-six set to make up the pattern shown. Patterns of this kind, where the numbers of spots on adjacent dominoes occur in square blocks made from four half dominoes, were named *quadrilles* by the French mathematician Edouard Lucas in the nineteenth century. Quadrilles can be made using all of the 28 dominoes in a standard double-six set. Three such patterns are shown in outline below, where each has fourteen squares equivalent to four half dominoes with the same number of spots. There are many solutions to each, but can you find one?

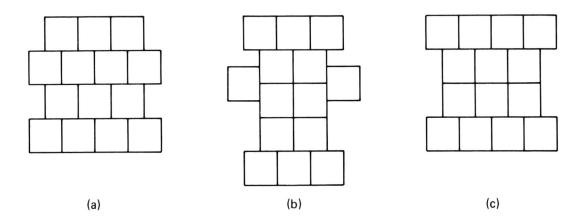

(a)   (b)   (c)

Can you make a quadrille in the shape of a square or rectangle from a subset of dominoes?

86 Subtraction to addition

Learning to subtract two numbers, sooner or later leads to problems of borrowing or paying back. But it need not be the case. The method of complementary addition about to be described, ensures that whenever subtraction occurs, a digit is always taken from 9, so that no borrowing is called for.

Suppose, for example, we need to take 489 from 573 then we make life easy for ourselves by taking 489 from 999 instead, to give 510. Next we *add* 510 to 573 giving 1083, and finally we ignore the 1 in the thousands column, but add 1 to the units column to give a final answer of 84.

$$
\begin{array}{c}
-\ \begin{array}{r} 573 \\ 489 \\ \hline \end{array}
\end{array}
\quad \text{first} \quad
\begin{array}{c}
-\ \begin{array}{r} 999 \\ 489 \\ \hline 510 \end{array}
\end{array}
\quad \text{second} \quad
\begin{array}{c}
+\ \begin{array}{r} 573 \\ 510 \\ \hline 1083 \end{array}
\end{array}
$$

then finally $\not1083 + 1 = 84$.

Here is another example to clarify the method:

$$
\begin{array}{c}
-\ \begin{array}{r} 35\ 274 \\ 18\ 596 \\ \hline \end{array}
\end{array}
\quad \text{first} \quad
\begin{array}{c}
-\ \begin{array}{r} 99\ 999 \\ 18\ 596 \\ \hline 81\ 403 \end{array}
\end{array}
\quad \text{second} \quad
\begin{array}{c}
+\ \begin{array}{r} 35\ 274 \\ 81\ 403 \\ \hline 116\ 677 \end{array}
\end{array}
$$

then finally $\not116\ 677 + 1 = 16\ 678$

Check these subtractions using conventional methods or a calculator, then try out the method for yourself on sums of your own choosing.

Now explain why the method works.

87 Start with any digit

(a) Take any digit and use your calculator to multiply it by 239, and the product so formed by 4649.
What do you observe?
Why does it work?
Could you get the same result by multiplying your choice of digit by any other two whole numbers?

(b) Take any digit and multiply it in turn by 73, then 11, then 101, then 137. Explain the result.

88 What route should the ant take?

When an ant, A, is 25 cm from a cylindrical glass beaker it spots a drop of honey at C inside the far side of the beaker and 6 cm below its rim. If the circumference of the beaker is 16 cm, and it stands 9 cm high, what is the shortest route for the ant to reach the honey?

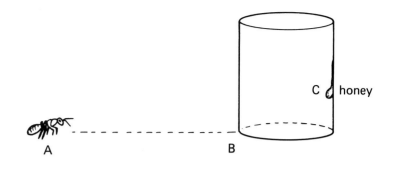

89 What were the stamps?

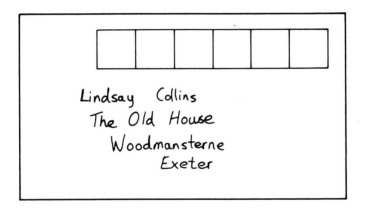

Lindsay is a keen stamp collector. One day she received a letter from one of her overseas contacts with six stamps in a line across the top of the envelope. The total face value of all the stamps came to 160 cents, but what intrigued Lindsay was the way the stamps were arranged. On close inspection, she saw that she could choose a single stamp, or a set of neighbouring stamps, which added up to every one of the following totals:

   10 c, 20 c, 30 c, 40 c, . . . , 160 c

Given that the left-hand stamp had a lower face value than the right-hand stamp, what were the face values of the six stamps?

90　Vandalised!

A barge loaded with iron ingots was moored in a canal lock overnight. Unfortunately for the owners some late night revellers decided to empty all the iron overboard into the lock. What happens to the water level in the lock as a result of dumping all the iron? Assume the lock doesn't leak!

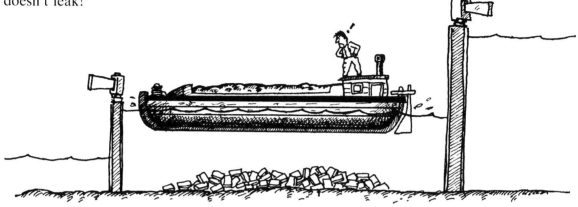

91　A calculator conundrum

Work out

$$\sqrt{1.2.3.4 + 1}$$
$$\sqrt{2.3.4.5 + 1}$$
$$\sqrt{3.4.5.6 + 1}$$
$$\sqrt{4.5.6.7 + 1}$$

What do you notice?
Try with four larger consecutive numbers to see what happens. It is very easy to select numbers beyond the capacity of your calculator. What happens then?

92　The ship's masts

Two ship's masts are of height 6 m and 4 m respectively. Guy wires are stretched from the top of each to the base of the other as shown. The wires cross at a height of 2.4 m above the deck.

　　How far apart are the masts?

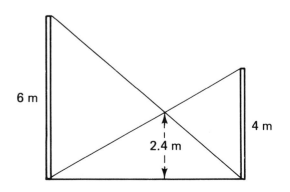

93 Help the book designer

A book designer wants to improve the layout of a new book. She is required to have a rectangular block of text of area 216 cm², and wants to surround this with margins down each side of 2 cm, a head margin of 3 cm, and a foot margin of 3 cm. To save on paper costs she wants to minimise the area of each page. What dimensions should she make the pages?

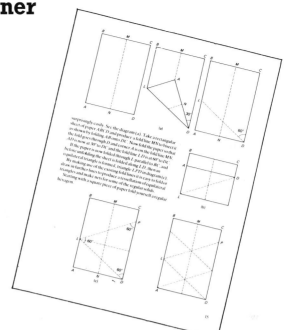

94 Orienteering

Two orienteering competitors Peter and Ada arrived at control *A* together but left it in opposite directions in their search for control *B*. Peter headed due south for 150 metres before heading due east, where he found control *B* after running a further 600 metres. Ada meanwhile started out in a northerly direction before changing to a bearing which took her straight to *B*. Interestingly both competitors had covered the same distance in their routes from *A* to *B*.

How far north did Ada run before changing direction?

95 The circular square balance

In the ten-spoked wheel shown, four of the circles already
have numbers inserted and these have the property that
the sum of the squares of two adjacent numbers equals the
sum of the squares of the two opposite numbers:

$$2^2 + 49^2 = 2405 = 14^2 + 47^2$$

What is intriguing, is that whole numbers can be found to
put in each of the other eight circles so that this same
property is maintained for every pair of adjacent numbers
on the rim of the wheel. Can you find them?

To encourage you, no other number is larger than 26.
Oh, and of course, no two numbers are the same!

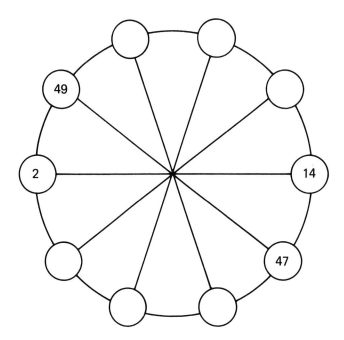

96 The cranky calculator

An electronic calculator has all its digit keys and its
memory key working efficiently but the only function keys
still working reliably are

Devise a routine which enables you to find the product of
any two numbers within the capacity of the calculator.

97 Two squares to one

On a piece of paper draw two squares next to each other as shown. Their relative sizes are not important. Now draw two straight lines to divide the figure into four pieces which can be fitted together as a jigsaw to form a single square.

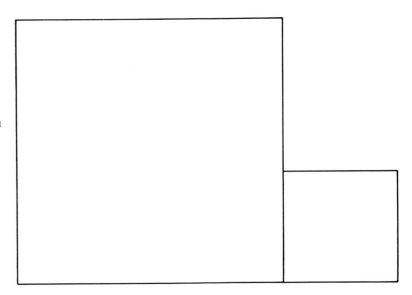

98 Self motivated!

Judy and Nigel were keen to get to a pop festival at a town 21 miles away, but having missed the bus they would have to make their own way. Judy was a keen cyclist and could speed along on her cycle at 16 mph. Nigel didn't own a cycle, but reckoned he could average 12 mph on Judy's cycle. Judy can jog at 6 mph quite happily, while Nigel considers himself a runner and can jog at 8 mph for many a mile.

How should they arrange their journey so that they leave home together and arrive at the festival together in the shortest possible time, by a mixture of jogging and sharing the bicycle?

99 Satisfying the Sultan's wives!

The Sultan had four young wives who would surely outlive him, so in his will he devised a plan to leave them each a portion of his land. The piece of land he had in mind to share between them was in the shape of an isosceles trapezium where the parallel sides were 10 km apart, and of lengths 10 km and 30 km. Never a straightforward person, the Sultan decreed that his wives should share out the land in the following way:

His first wife is to erect a flagpole on the land, the second, third and fourth wives, in turn, may then choose a triangular portion of the land with one vertex at the flagpole and the other two on the boundary of the trapezium. The first wife will then inherit what the other wives have not laid claim to. How should the first wife place the flagpole to maximise her own inheritance and minimise that of the others?

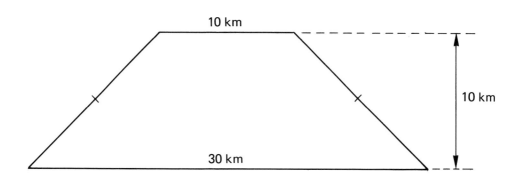

100 Complete the tetrahedron

All the faces of a tetrahedron have the same area. Two of its edges are known to be of length 5 cm and 6 cm. What are the lengths of the other four remaining edges?

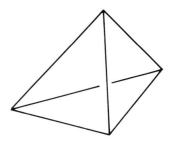

52

101   Help the bosun

The hold of a cargo ship contained ten large crates packed as shown. At their first port of call the only crate needing to be off-loaded was *A*, the largest. Unfortunately, because of the position and size of the hatch to this hold it is only possible to off-load *A* if it is in the middle of the opposite end of the hold. The ship's captain foresaw the problem while they were still at sea and set his bosun the task of rearranging the crates. In the confines of the hold it is only possible to slide the crates without turning them or lifting them over one another. The bosun has quite a problem on his hands, can you help him?

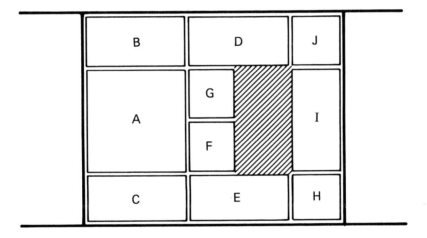

102   Only 'takes' and 'adds'

Write down the digits 9 to 1 in descending order, and by suitably interposing + and − signs form a sum which totals 100. For example:

$$98 - 7 + 6 + 5 + 4 - 3 - 2 - 1 = 100$$

There are a surprising number of ways of achieving the century without using any other signs, not even brackets.
   How many ways can you find?
   Can you achieve the century using only *four* signs?

103 Fox and geese

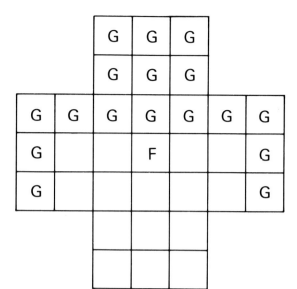

This is a game for two players played on a squared board in the shape of a cross as shown. You will need seventeen counters to represent the geese and these are placed in the squares marked *G* in the diagram. One more counter of a different colour or size can then be used for the fox who starts at the square marked *F*, in the centre.

The geese can move one square at a time either left, right or down but not up or diagonally.

The fox can move one cell at a time either left, right, up or down. Further, it can jump over a goose (and remove it), if the goose is in its path and the square on the other side of the goose is vacant.

The object of the game is for the geese to surround the fox so that it cannot move, while the fox tries to consume the geese and avoid capture. The geese have the first move.

Play the game and see if you can devise a winning strategy.

This is typical of many games originating in northern Europe in the thirteenth century, where the numbers of pieces controlled by each player, and their objectives, are different. The earliest English reference to the game is in the accounts of the royal household of Edward IV, but much earlier references can be found in Iceland.

104 Calculator contortions

To test the ingenuity of her bright pupils, Mrs Challenger set them the potentially dreary task of working out a long list of multiplications. But to help them she gave them each a calculator which had been especially modified so that the only keys still operational were the digit keys, the memory, and the function keys $\boxed{+}$, $\boxed{-}$ and $\boxed{1/x}$. After an hour most of her pupils were defeated and resorted to long multiplication, but long before this Betty Bolzano, the form genius, had produced all the correct answers using one of the calculators. How did she do it?

105 The magician's ribbon factory

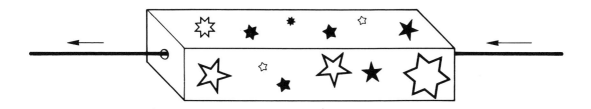

A magician asked his supplier of tricks if they could design a trick for him which would appear to manufacture ribbon. His supplier came up with a star-spangled box which had a small hole in each end. A piece of ribbon appeared to enter the box through one hole and come out through the opposite hole but in such a way that it emerged at *three* times the rate at which it went in!

Could you design such a box?

106 Domino Latin squares

1	2	3	4
2	3	4	1
3	4	1	2
4	1	2	3

1	2	3	4	5
2	3	4	5	1
3	4	5	1	2
4	5	1	2	3
5	1	2	3	4

Any $n \times n$ square array of numbers where each row and column contains each of the n numbers 1 to n once only, as in the examples above, is called a Latin square.

Can you make up any Latin squares using a standard double-six set of dominoes?

107 Star puzzle 3

The numbers 1 to 12 have been arranged in the star so that the totals of the five numbers along the six lines a, b, c, d, e, and f are either 29 or 30.

There are many ways in which the numbers can be arranged so that half the lines total one number and half another. See what you can find.

The challenge proposed here is to find an arrangement of the numbers where the totals along a, b, c, d, e and f form a consecutive set of numbers.

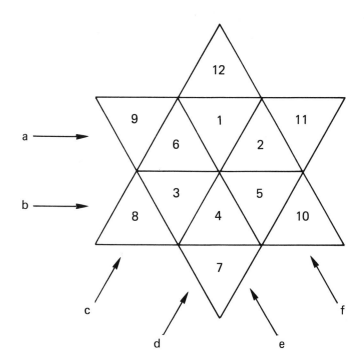

108 The medieval courtyard

A medieval monastry was built around a courtyard in the form of a square. In the courtyard was the well from which the monks obtained all their drinking water. The well was so placed that its distance from three consecutive corners was 30 m, 40 m and 50 m respectively.

How big was the courtyard?

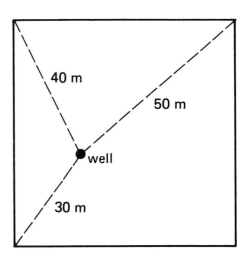

109 A Russian two-step

In the past Russian peasants supposedly used a method of multiplication, which only required knowledge of the two times table. The method consisted of systematically halving one of the numbers being multiplied and doubling the other. Suppose, for example, we want to find the product of 39 and 79, then we proceed as follows:

	39	79	←
39 × 79	19	158	←
	9	316	←
	4	632	
	2	1264	
	1	2528	←

Form two columns headed by 39 and 79. Divide the last number entered in the left-hand column by two and, ignoring any remainder, enter the result in this column. Now multiply the last number in the right-hand column by two and put the result in that column. Continue this halving and doubling process until the last number in the left column is 1.

Finally, add together all those numbers in the right-hand column which come opposite an odd number in the left-hand column (shown arrowed). The sum of these numbers gives the required product:

39 × 79 = 79 + 158 + 316 + 2528 = 3081

Try out this method for yourself on other numbers and check the correctness of the product using a calculator or other means.

Can you explain why the method works?

110 Crossed ladders

In an alleyway between two houses two ladders are leaning against the walls as shown.

AB is 8 m long
CD is 10 m long

The ladders cross at a height of 4 m above the ground. How far apart are the houses?

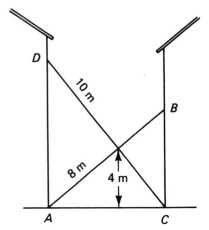

57

111 Political planning

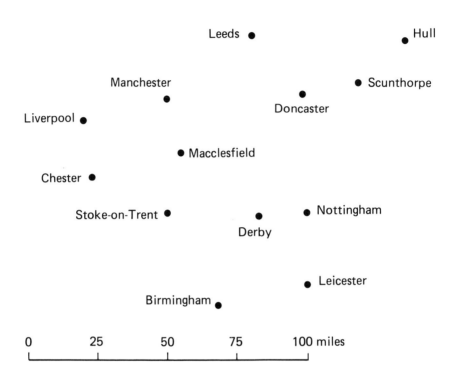

The leader of a certain political party, hoping to boost his party's chances at the general election, plans to tour all the towns on the map shown. To cut down his travelling time he arranges to hire a helicopter, but to conserve his party's limited funds he needs to optimise the total distance travelled between the towns. Starting and ending at Birmingham what route should he take?

112 The prime gaps

Counting from 1 to 100 it is not far from one prime number to the next, but as you count on past 100 some of the gaps from one prime to the next are surprisingly large. Between 1000 and 2000, for example, there are five gaps of 20 or more without a prime. Use a computer or table of prime numbers to see how large a gap you can find.

113 Birthday products

Mary was delighted on her fifteenth birthday,
    13 July 1991 (13/7/91)
when she realised that the product of the day of the
month together with the month in the year, was equal to
the year in the century:
    13 × 7 = 91
She started thinking about other occasions in the century
when such an event might occur, and imagine her surprise
when she realised that her two younger brothers would
encounter a similar relationship on their fifteenth
birthdays also. Given that their birthdays are on
consecutive days, when were they all born?

114 Dante's division

Dante Dallas, the eccentric oil billionaire, devised a
scheme to share out his 84 billion dollar fortune between
his three children. He asked them each to find a triangle
whose sides were of integer length, and whose area was 84
square units. Then, no matter how many such triangles
they found, he would put their details in a hat and draw
one. The lengths of the sides of the triangle so drawn
would then be used as the ratio to divide up his
inheritance, with his eldest child receiving the largest sum,
and so on.

  In the event each of his children presented him with a
different triangle. As a result of the draw the two older
children were disappointed, but the youngest was elated!
What were the dimensions of the three triangles, and what
did they each inherit?

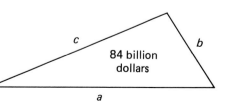

59

115   How long was the sermon?

The Reverend Verbose was renowned for the length of his sermons and the variety of his sentence lengths. But his daughters, forced to sit through them all were not amused. One day, to pass the time, they decided to count the number of words in each sentence of his sermon. They were intrigued to find that he had used every sentence length from 1 to N words, and that the frequency with which each length was used was inversely proportional to its length. He had used: N single-word sentences, $(N-1)$ two-word sentences, $(N-2)$ three-word sentences, and so on up to 1 sentence with N words. If on average each word took a second, and the sermon was almost 2 hours long, what is the length of his longest sentence?

116   The square touch

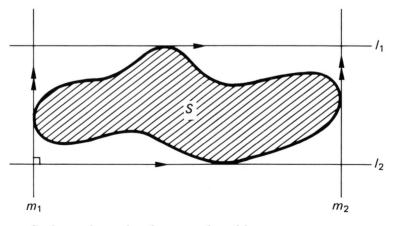

The shaded shape S, shown here, has been enclosed by two pairs of parallel lines, all of which touch S, and are at right angles so that they form a rectangle.

Is it possible to find a square enclosing S whose sides also touch it?

117 This tetraflexagon has six faces

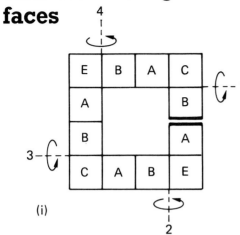

(i)

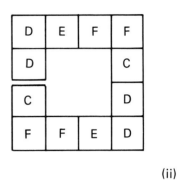

(ii)

Four-sided paper structures made from strips of paper which can be folded to expose different surfaces are known as tetraflexagons. The one discussed here can be folded to expose any one of six faces denoted here by A, B, C, D, E, F. Made with care it gives an intriguing object to manipulate. Instead of the same letter repeated four times on each exposed surface a message of four letter words can be sent, such as:

LILY WITH MUCH LOVE FROM JOHN

To make this flexagon carefully draw the band of twelve squares shown in figure (i) on plain paper. (A 3-cm edge to each square is appropriate.)

Letter the band as shown in (i), cut it out, turn it over and letter the underside as shown in (ii). Where the band has been cut between A and B the cut edges have been marked with a double line, for they will later be stuck together.

Carefully fold the band along each of the edges of the squares so that it flexes easily. (If card is used then score all the fold lines.) Return the band to the configuration shown in (i) and fold it along the dotted lines in the order indicated. In each case fold under. The result should look like (iii).

Now fold as indicated in (iii) where the first and third folds are up over, and the second fold is under. At the third fold tuck C behind A so the result looks like (iv) and the reverse side like (v).

Use a piece of sticky tape to join the top edge of the A to the edge of the B behind as shown. These should be the edges marked in (i). By folding along the horizontal mediator you will now be able to expose any of A, B, C, D and by folding along the vertical mediator find E and F.

Have fun!

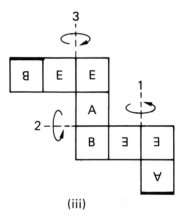

(iii)

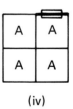

(iv)

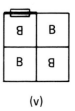

(v)

118 A cautionary tale

To give his class practice in using calculators a mathematics teacher set them to solve the simultaneous equations

$$32.26x + 14.95y = 28.35$$
$$187.3x + 79.43y = 83.29$$

He hadn't worked out the solution himself because he had taken the question from a textbook for which he had the answers. Unfortunately he had misread one of the coefficients and given the class 14.95 where the book had 14.96. He realised his mistake well into the lesson, but argued with himself that such a small change could hardly affect the answer. Only when the children's work came in and the brightest girls had answers which agreed with each other but looked very different from those in his book did he work out both sets of solutions for himself. What did he find? Was the book wrong? Were the girls wrong? Could both be right? Investigate and try to account for your findings.

119 The wine importer

A wine importer was pleased to receive a large consignment of bottles of wine from his favourite French vineyard, and immediately celebrated by drinking one of the bottles. The next day after receiving the wine he sold exactly a fifth of the remaining bottles, which was a good enough excuse to treat himself to a second bottle. Sales continued to flourish. On the third day he again sold exactly one fifth of the bottles he had in stock at the beginning of the day. So again he celebrated with a bottle for himself. This pattern continued until the end of the seventh day, when the number of bottles left no longer made it possible for him to dispose of a fifth of them on the eighth day.

How many bottles did the wine importer have in his consignment?

120 Area equals perimeter

A circle of radius 2 and a square of side 4 have the interesting property that their areas are numerically equal to their perimeters. Are there any other shapes with this property? See what you can find.

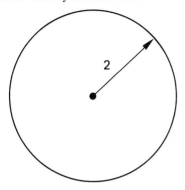

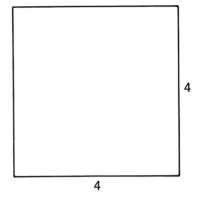

121 Fix the watch towers

The Forestry Commission owned a plantation of fir trees in the shape of a triangle, ABC. The sides of the triangle had lengths as follows: $AB = 975$ m, $BC = 845$ m, $CA = 910$ m. It is required to build three watch towers for fire prevention purposes so that there is one tower on each side of the triangle. The Forestry Commission also wish to join each tower directly to each other by a straight path which will act as a fire-break as well as an easy means of communication. But making the paths is expensive, as well as wasteful of space, so it is important to place the towers at points P, Q and R to minimise the length of

$PQ + QR + RP$

Where should the watch towers be placed?

122 Truncating primes

The number 73 939 133 has the fascinating property that not only is it prime, but as the least-significant digit is successively chopped off, the remaining numbers are also prime, namely

7 393 913, 739 391, 73 939, 7393, 739, 73, 7

73 939 133 is the largest number with the property, and clearly all the numbers formed by truncating it also have the same property. The challenge is to find all such numbers.

123 Robotic rovings

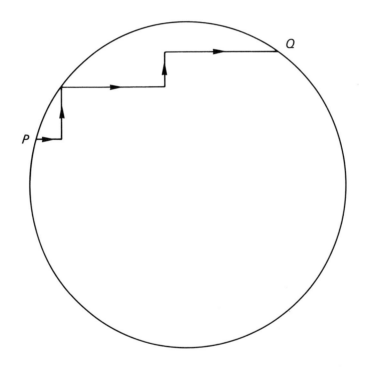

A robot is free to move around inside a circular boundary of radius 10 m. However, it is programmed in such a way that it can only move from left to right and upwards. See the figure. It changes direction at random, or when it reaches the boundary. Eventually it will meet the boundary at a point where no further progress is possible, at which point it switches itself off. What is the longest route possible for the robot? (You may ignore the physical dimensions of the robot for this exercise!)

124 Climbing Mt Igneous

Mt Igneous rises from a flat plain in the typical shape, for an active volcano, of the frustum of a cone. A team of volcanologists set out from a camp at the base of the volcano at *A* with the intention of trekking to the diametrically opposite point *B* by the shortest route. The base of the volcano has a diameter of 2 km, and its surface slopes upwards at 60°, while the shortest distance from *A* to the edge of the volcanic crater is 1 km.

How far do they need to travel?

What would be the shortest route for the team if they also want to reach the crater's edge en route from *A* to *B*?

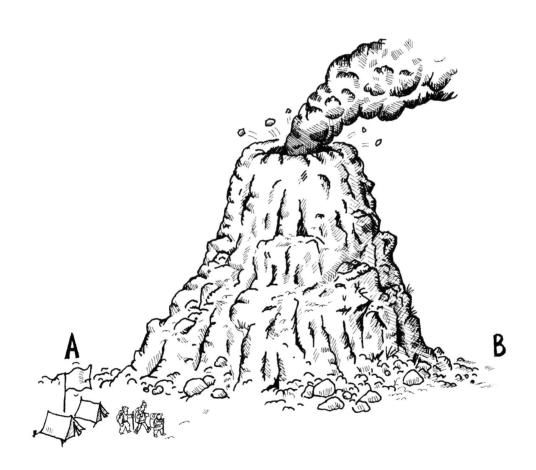

125 Round and around

Look at the very special pattern in these divisions

$$4\overline{)615\,384} \qquad 4\overline{)410\,256}$$
$$153\,846 \qquad 102\,564$$

The quotient appears to be obtained by moving the left-hand digit to the right-hand end of the number being divided by 4.

The question arises, 'Are these numbers unique?'. You can soon prove to yourself that they are not, by completing the following so that the same pattern holds

$$4\overline{)92*\,***} \qquad 4\overline{)3**\,***}$$
$$23*\,*** \qquad ***\,**3$$

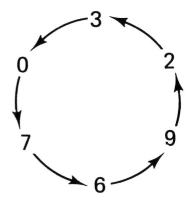

Notice how in both these cases the order of the digits is the same when they are thought of as continuous cycles.

Now complete the following in the same way

$$4\overline{)8**\,***} \qquad 4\overline{)5**\,***} \qquad 4\overline{)2**\,***}$$
$$***\,**8 \qquad ***\,**5 \qquad ***\,**2$$

So far only division by 4 has been encountered. Can similar patterns be found when dividing by other numbers? Consider division by 2 for example:

$$2\overline{)315\,789\,473\,684\,210\,526}$$
$$157\,894\,736\,842\,105\,263$$

This time a cycle of 18 digits was needed before the required pattern could be achieved

Try completing the following:

$$2\overline{)5} \qquad 2\overline{)7} \qquad 2\overline{)9}$$

What do you notice?

Investigate the length of the cycle needed to achieve the pattern when dividing by 3.

Can you explain the results?

126 Pythagorean triples

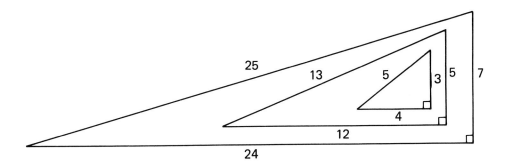

The mathematics teacher gave her annual lesson to year 10 about Pythagorean triples, whole numbers a, b, and c which satisfy the relation $a^2 + b^2 = c^2$, and could be used as the sides of right-angled triangles. She then gave them the three examples shown and optimistically set a homework to find further examples.

She was taken aback next day when Miranda not only reported that she had found a way of finding all such triples, but that she reckoned that at least one number in every such triple would be divisible by 5. However she wanted a proof of her conjecture . . ..

127 Tape recorder teaser

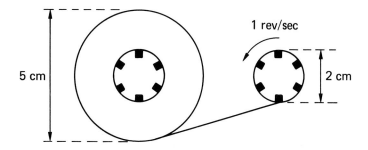

Observation of a typical cassette tape recorder suggests that the drive to the take-up reel rotates at approximately one revolution a second. When a C60 cassette starts to play the diameter of the empty reel is 2 cm, and when it comes to an end after half an hour, the full reel has a diameter of 5 cm.

What is the thickness and length of the tape?
When is the tape travelling at a speed of 11 cms^{-1}?

128 Achilles and the tortoise

The infinite is a concept which has confused many people through the ages. As long ago as the fifth century BC the Greek philosopher Zeno highlighted the difficulty of this concept by proposing a number of paradoxes – self-contradictory statements. One of these argues that Achilles, the legendary athlete, could never overtake the slowest tortoise if the tortoise was given a head start.

The argument goes that Achilles must always first reach the point from which the tortoise has just departed, and in that time the tortoise will have moved on.

Experience tells us that there must be a flaw in the argument, but where does it lie?

129 Form your conclusion

Lewis Carroll is widely known for his books about Alice, but in practice he was an Oxford logician. The following ten statements are attributable to him and you are invited to deduce the unique conclusion which they all contribute to!

1 The only animals in this house are cats.
2 Every animal is suitable for a pet, that loves to gaze at the moon.
3 When I detest an animal, I avoid it.
4 No animals are carnivorous, unless they prowl at night.
5 No cat fails to kill mice.
6 No animals ever talk to me, except what are in this house.
7 Kangaroos are not suitable for pets.
8 None but carnivora kill mice.
9 I detest animals that do not talk to me.
10 Animals that prowl at night always love to gaze at the moon.

130 Surakarta

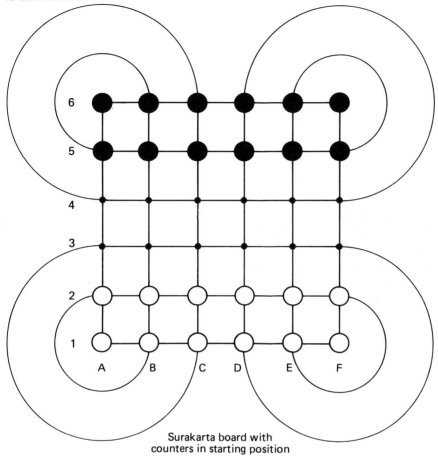

Surakarta board with
counters in starting position

Surakarta is an Indonesian game for two players named after the town in Java where it originated and it deserves to be better known. The board consists of a network of squares with interconnecting arcs of circles at the corners as shown above. Each player has twelve counters of a distinguishable colour and they are set out facing each other in two ranks of 6 at the start of the game. The players draw lots or spin a coin to see who starts, then take turns moving one piece at a time.

A *move* consists of moving a counter along a line *or* diagonally to an adjacent vacant point so, for example, at the start the piece on C2 can move to B3 or C3 or D3.

The object of the game is to capture one's opponent's pieces, and this is where the circular arcs come into play. A piece can only capture another piece when it has a clear path along the lines on the board, which must include a circular arc (or arcs) to that piece. When this is the case a piece can travel any distance along this path and ends up in the position of the opponent's piece which is removed from the board.

69

Diagrams (a) and (b) show several examples of capture.

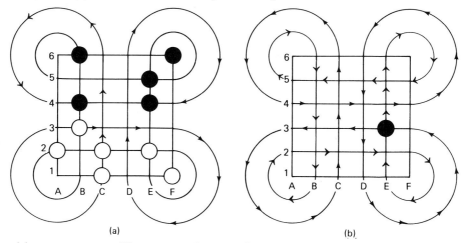

(a)   (b)

In (a) the white counter on C2 can travel up to C6, around the circle and along line 4 to capture the black counter on B4. The white counter on B3, although adjacent to the black counter on B4 cannot capture it as all routes between them which involve circles are blocked by other pieces.

However, the counter on B3 can move to the right along line 3, around the circular arc, up line D, around a second circular arc to capture the black counter on E4.

Note that all paths are two-way so that if white is in a position to capture black then black would also be able to capture white.

The circular paths, which can only be traversed when capturing an opponent's piece, are a unique feature of this game and give it a special interest.

Figure (b) illustrates the powerful attacking position of a point such as E3. By travelling up or down initially the path connects all the smaller circles, while by moving sideways initially all the lines connecting the large circles are accessible – always supposing there is no piece in the way. The potential of such a position to capturing opponent's pawns however is also its vulnerability to being attacked. The only positions on the board which are free from attack are the points at the centres of the circles.

The winner is the player who first reduces his opponent's 'army' to an agreed number, *or* the player with the largest 'army' on the board when time is called.

Draw yourself a board on a piece of card and try it out. You will need eyes like a hawk to watch those attacks coming from all sides!

For a more permanent board mark out the network on a piece of plywood and drill holes at the points to take coloured pegs.

131 Insights into the icosahedron

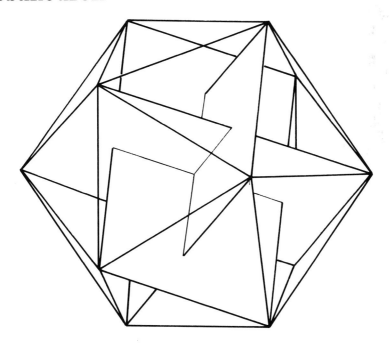

When a pair of opposite edges of an icosahedron are joined they form a rectangle whose sides are in the ratio of the golden section (approximately 1.618). If three such identical rectangles are cut out of card and slotted together symmetrically as shown above then their twelve vertices lie at the vertices of a regular icosahedron.

To make an icosahedron in this way use thick card and rectangles of say 13 cm by 8 cm (consecutive numbers in a Fibonacci sequence make a good approximation to the golden section ratio; see for example *Mathematical Activities* p. 127). Cut slits in the cards to slot them together and then use coloured wool or shirring elastic to complete the edges. A small notch at each corner will help to fix these edges securely.

The American genius Buckminster Fuller made a particular study of structures consisting of struts and tensioning wires and is famous for his designs of geodesic domes. Much of this study was concerned with minimum structures for keeping a given number of points fixed in place in space and the drawing (b) shows his solution for the twelve vertices of a regular icosahedron. It consists of six equal struts in compression, which lie in the positions represented by the long edges of the card rectangles in the earlier model, together with wire or nylon thread connecting their ends, in tension.

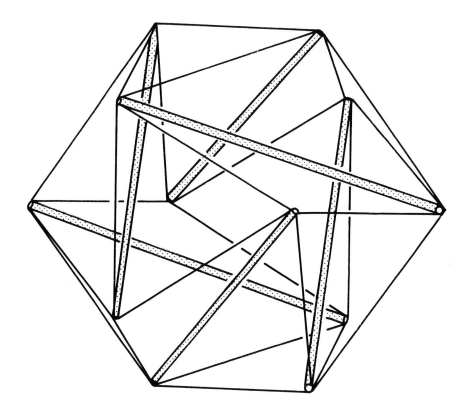

The drawing may appear to have some lines missing, for Buckminster Fuller discovered he did not need wires corresponding to all the edges of the icosahedron to keep his struts rigid. If you look carefully you will see four wires connecting the top of each strut in contrast to the five edges of a complete icosahedron at each vertex – but this makes the model all the more fascinating.

The model is not as difficult to make as it might first appear. Start by getting some 6 mm dowel rod and cutting from it six struts each 30 cm long. Next with a saw make a narrow cut 5 mm deep into the end of each strut. The struts are then joined together using six loops of string or nylon cord. The length of cord in each loop is critical, and with the struts here each loop such as *ABCD* and *PQRS* in the diagram should be 72 cm long when in tension. To achieve this make your loops by tying them tightly around a piece of card or hardboard which is 36 cm wide.

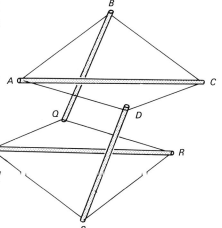

It is important for ease of construction of the model that the cord used fits tightly in the saw cuts at the ends of the struts so that they stay in place when not under tension.

First fit four struts and two loops together as shown above and then use the four remaining loops to add in the last two struts.

This is a very satisfying model to build and display.

Commentary

1 One square less

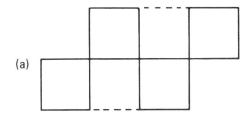

(a)

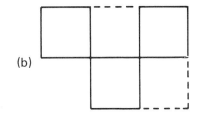

(b)

2 Only one left

Numbering the coins 1 to 9, as shown, and using the notation $x \uparrow y$ for x jumps over y, then one solution is given by

$$5 \uparrow 8, 5 \uparrow 9, 5 \uparrow 3,$$
$$5 \uparrow 1, 6 \uparrow 2, 7 \uparrow 4,$$
$$6 \uparrow 7, 5 \uparrow 6$$

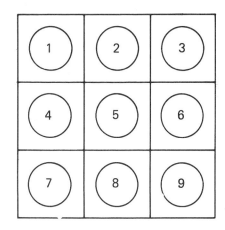

3 The eight pawns problem

One solution is shown here. Many other solutions are possible.

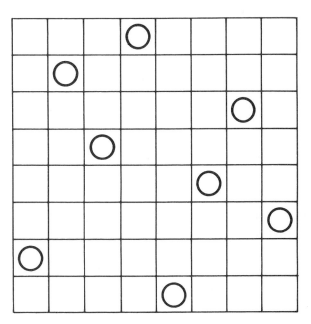

4 Pinball pursuits

The routes shown give the maximum totals, but there may
be other routes which also give the maximum totals.

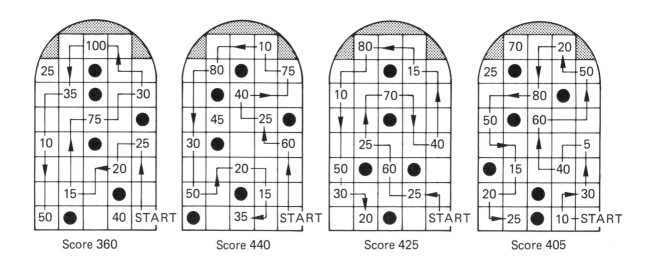

Score 360   Score 440   Score 425   Score 405

6 Pinboard crosses

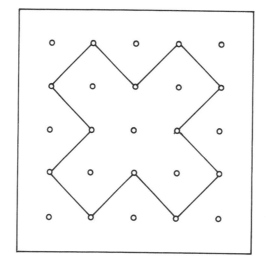

7 Be thrifty!

$$
\begin{array}{r}
9486 \\
+1076 \\
\hline
10562
\end{array}
\qquad
\begin{array}{r}
9476 \\
+1086 \\
\hline
10562
\end{array}
\qquad
\begin{array}{r}
9386 \\
+1076 \\
\hline
10462
\end{array}
\qquad
\begin{array}{r}
9376 \\
+1086 \\
\hline
10462
\end{array}
$$

8 The apprentice's task

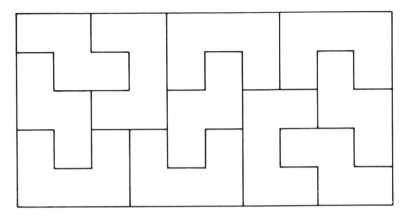

9 Catherine wheels

The two solutions shown here have been chosen because they are in a sense the reverse of each other; the numbers along the spokes of the one on the left are the numbers along the spirals of the one on the right, and vice versa. Anyone familiar with magic squares will see the connection.

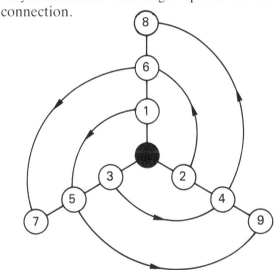

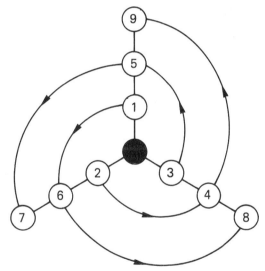

10 The intruder

The safe is in room D.

Replace the room plan by a network in the following way. Put a node in the middle of each room and a node for the corridor. Next draw arcs between the nodes to correspond to each internal doorway. The result will be as shown. As the intruder passed once through each doorway this is equivalent to travelling along each arc of the network once. Having started at F, an odd node, he or she must end at the only other odd node in the network, namely D.

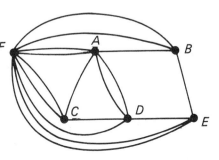

11 An unfortunate snag

x	1	$11 - x$
$15 - 2x$	4	$2x - 7$
$x - 3$	7	$8 - x$

4	1	7
7	4	1
1	7	4

5	1	6
5	4	3
2	7	3

6.5	1	4.5
2	4	6
3.5	7	1.5

Let the top left-hand cell contain the number x, then as the centre cell contains 4 the magic total is 12 and the numbers in the other cells are as shown in the diagram. If all the entries are to be positive then $3.5 < x < 7.5$. The only whole numbers satisfying this inequality are 4, 5, 6, 7 and lead to the solutions found by the children. So the only way to satisfy Ms Mehta is to choose, for example, $x = 6.5$ giving the square shown.

12 Grannie Stitchwork's teddy bears

She made only five teddy bears!

Doubling the linear dimensions increases the surface area 4 times, and the volume by a factor of 8, so 20 large teddy bears would require 24 m^2 of fur, 40 kg of kapok, and 8 m of ribbon.

13 Which is the best route?

The smallest number of moves to achieve more than 500 is 12. The following sequence of numbers totals 501:

24 14 42 34 58 11 50 64 48 55 32 69

The probability of anyone achieving this is small – $\left(\frac{1}{4}\right)^{12}$.

15 Square the vase

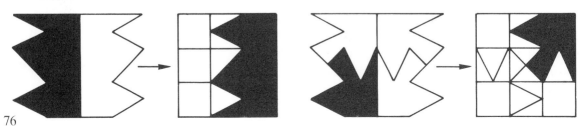

16 The newsboy's Sunday exertions

2030 metres.

Peter can travel from H to A (250 m) then go to D (180 m) then traverse the whole network and end at H. One of the many optimum solutions is as follows:

$H\,E\,F\,I\,A\,B\,D\,C\,B\,D\,J\,B\,A\,J\,I\,A\,G\,I\,F\,G\,H\,E\,F\,J\,E\,D\,H.$

17 The Josephus problem

Josephus placed himself and his friend in the thirty-first and sixteenth positions in the circle of people.

18 A magic domino square

The magic total is 10.

Try making up other magic squares using a set of dominoes.

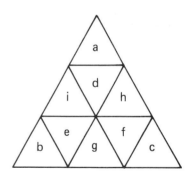

19 Triangular number patterns

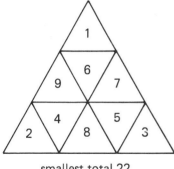

smallest total 22

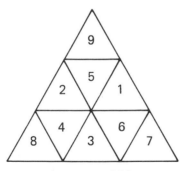

largest total 28

Examples giving the smallest and largest possible totals are shown. From a given solution, seven others can be easily found by realising that interchanging any or all of $a \longleftrightarrow d$, $b \longleftrightarrow e$, $c \longleftrightarrow f$ will leave the totals unchanged. In investigating this pattern it is helpful to appreciate the different roles of the three underlying patterns represented by the positions of (a, b, c), (d, e, f) and (g, h, i).

Did you manage to find patterns for the totals in between, that is 23, 24, 26 and 27?

20 A two touching transformation

To change the H to the square:

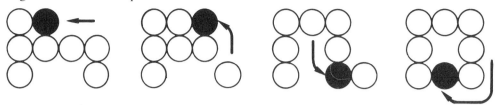

Here is one solution for transforming the square to an H in seven moves. If you find a shorter solution the author would like to hear from you!

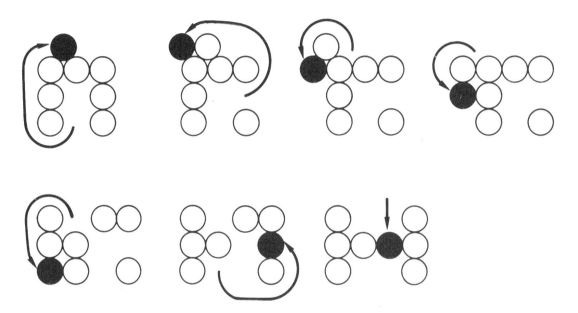

21 Knight's Solitaire

Using a co-ordinate system based on 1 to 5, and A to E, as shown, a solution in 38 moves sent by Irene Domingo from Brunei, where the co-ordinates indicate the piece being moved, is as follows:

4E 2D 4C 3A 1B 3C 1D 3E 2C 4B 5D 3C 4A 5C 3B
1A 2C 4D 3B 1C 3D 1E 2C 4B 2A 1C 2E 4D 3B 5A
4C 5E 3D 2B 4C 3A 5B 3C

If you find a better solution the author would like to hear from you.

22 Matchstick magic

23 Coaxial contortions

The 30° is a detractor. Imagine part of a net for the building including the roofs and relevant walls. Then the straight line from A to B corresponds to the shortest route. Its length is 15 m, easily shown by using Pythagoras' theorem. Then similar triangles give the point at which the cable leaves the sloping roof as 4.5 m from the end.

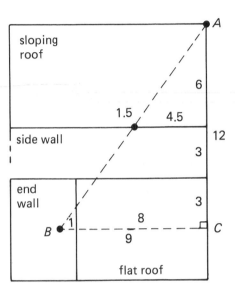

24 Double up!

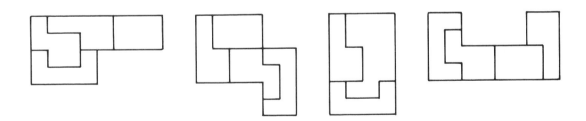

26 Wedding preparations

$$l + n = 132$$
$$n + s = 151$$
$$s + l = 137$$

adding gives $2(l + n + s) = 420$,

so $l + n + s = 210$

Subtracting the weight of each pair in turn from 210 gives the daughters' weights as

Louise 59 kg   Nancy 73 kg   Susannah 78 kg

27 Olive Orchard's cider measures

1 Fill the 7-litre measure, then pour into the 4-litre measure, leaving 3 litres in the 7-litre measure.
2 Empty the 4-litre measure into the barrel, then pour 3 litres from the 7-litre measure into the 4-litre measure.
3 Fill the 7-litre measure and pour 1 litre from it into the 4-litre measure to fill it leaving 6 litres.
4 Empty the 4-litre measure into the barrel, then pour 4 litres into it from the 7-litre measure, leaving 2 litres.

28 Star puzzle 1

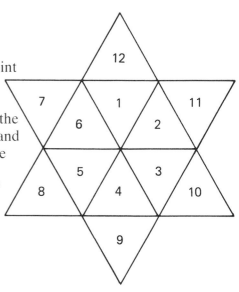

There are very many solutions, one is shown.
As $1 + 2 + 3 + 4 + \ldots + 12 = 78$, then the point-to-point total is $78 \div 3 = 26$. Pair off the numbers from 1 to 12 which total 13, such as, $12 + 1$, $11 + 2$, $10 + 3$, and so on. Now put these in the diamonds which radiate from the centre. These can be put in any order around the star, and further, the sequence of the four numbers which then lie on a diagonal connecting opposite points can be altered freely. There are thus very many solutions. How many?

29 Domino products

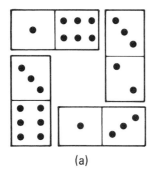

(a)

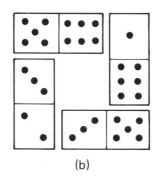

(b)

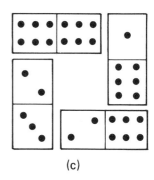

(c)

30 When was Jane born?

Jane was born in 1983.

Let David's and Jane's present ages be x and y.
Then $2x = 4(y + 5)$ and $x - 4 = 4(y - 4)$.
Solving the equations simultaneously gives $y = 11$.

32 Formation dancing

Three moves in each case:

(a)   MMMFFF → MMFMFF → MMFFMF → MFMFMF
(b)   MMMFFF → MFFFMM → MFF MFM → FMFMFM
   or MMMFFF → FFMMMF → FMF MMF → FMFMFM
   or MMMFFF → FFMMMF → FMF FMM → FMFMFM

33 The gardener's predicament

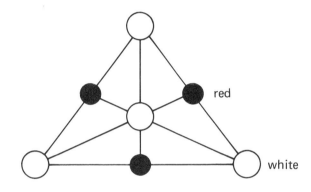

34 Fair shares for all

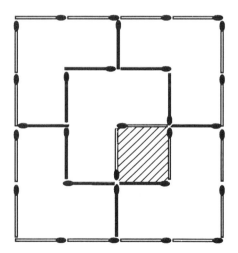

35 Count the trains

You would meet seventeen trains.
$1\frac{1}{2}$ hours = 90 mins = 9 × 10 mins so nine trains are on
the circuit coming towards you at the time you leave. In
the time it takes you to complete the circuit eight more
trains will have left Paddington on an anticlockwise
circuit, so you will meet seventeen trains in all.

36 Isoperimetric shapes

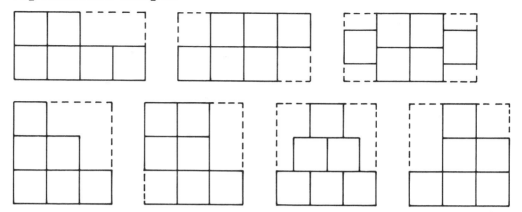

There are an infinite number of solutions if no constraint
is made on the way in which the tiles overlap. All these
solutions are related to the two given and can be obtained
from them by sliding tiles along their edges, as long as
(a) the shape so formed is bounded by a 4 × 2 rectangle,
   or 3 × 3 square, and
(b) in the sliding process two tiles are not slid apart from
   each other so as to expose additional edges.
A selection of solutions is shown above.

37 Number patterns

(a) The total is always of the form 711 . . . 117, as
   8 . . . 8888888 × 8 = 711 . . . 1111104, due to the fact
   that after the first two places a 7 digit is carried which
   together with 8 × 8 = 64 gives 71, leading to a put
   down digit of 1 and a further carry digit of 7.
(b) The pattern builds symmetrically in a very satisfying
   way: 1, 121, 12321, 1234321, . . . up to
   12345678987654321 and is easily understood by
   considering

$$
\begin{array}{r}
11111 \\
\times\ 11111 \\
\hline
111110000 \\
11111000 \\
1111100 \\
111110 \\
11111 \\
\hline
123454321
\end{array}
$$

But as soon as numbers involving ten or more units
digits are multiplied a carry is involved and the
pattern disintegrates in the middle.

38 Navigational hazards

Thirteen crossings are needed.

Let E and N represent the boatmen, and e and n represent the non-boatmen, then the diagram shows how the river crossing is achieved.

Eee Nnn	Nn → ← N	n
Eee Nn	Nn → ← N	nn
Eee N	Ee → ← En	en
Ee Nn	EN → ← En	Ne
Ee nn	Ee → ← N	Eee
N nn	Nn → ← N	Eee n
N n	Nn →	Eee Nnn

39 Square the goblet

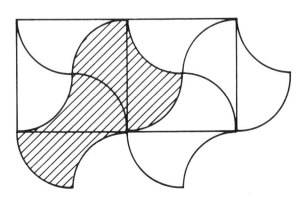

40 Reptiles!

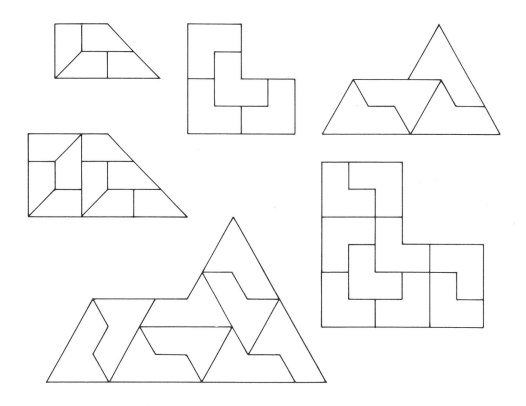

41 Turn Summer into Spring

Unique solution

```
    8432
+   8475
  ------
   16907
```

42 Four in a line

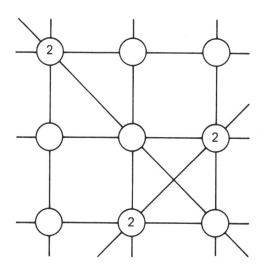

43   The ring main

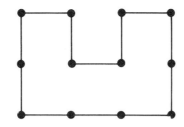

44   This looks easy!

Nine regions, as shown.

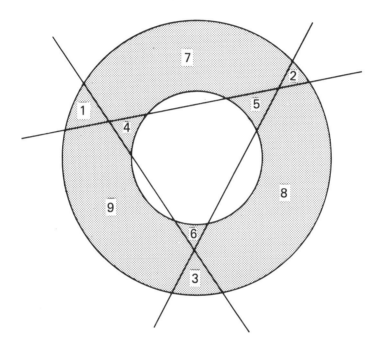

45   Have fun with a flexagon tube

This is surprisingly tricky. If you become really frustrated write to the author for a solution!

46   The giant and the dwarfs

With the given starting position the dwarfs should win by trapping the giant in circle 5, but one false move and he can slip past them.

With other starting positions the advantage can change in the giant's favour. For example, if the dwarfs start as in the diagram but the giant starts on square 1 then the giant should win. See if you can decide which starting positions ensure a win for the dwarfs (always assuming they use the right tactics) and which favour the giant.

47 Surprise, surprise!

$13 \times 7 \times 11 = 1001$

Hence $abc \times 13 \times 7 \times 11 = abc \times 1001$
$$= abc \times 1000 + abc$$
$$= abcabc$$

48 A kind of magic

The array is simply an addition table with the numbers bordering the table removed. The method for selecting the five numbers from the array ensures that each number bordering the original table is added in once, so the magic total is the sum of these ten numbers, 84.

Make your own version of the square. It can be smaller, or larger. The skill comes in trying to make all the numbers in the array different without the numbers becoming too large. Can you devise a 5×5 square with these properties where the magic total is less than 84?

+	5	1	14	0	10
8	13	9	22	8	18
19	24	20	33	19	29
0	5	1	14	0	10
25	30	26	39	25	35
2	7	3	16	2	12

49 How old was the Rev. Pascal?

To solve the problem it is necessary to consider sets of consecutive numbers which add up to 1000. This can be done by trial and error, or by making use of the formula

$$1 + 2 + 3 + \ldots + n = \tfrac{1}{2} n (n + 1)$$

If the Rev. Pascal is aged n years, and his wife aged m years on the day he retires, then

$$\tfrac{1}{2} n (n + 1) - \tfrac{1}{2} (m - 1)m = 1000$$

From which
$$n (n + 1) - (m - 1)m = 2000$$

This has three solutions, namely

$$(n, m) = (202, 198) \text{ or } (52, 28) \text{ or } (70, 55)$$

and the only numbers which fit the story line are $n = 70$ and $m = 55$. So on their wedding day the Rev. Pascal and his wife were 55 and 40 years old respectively.

51 The biker's challenge

The shortest routes must all start at Suziwich and end at Kawaport having traversed the sections from Yamapool to Harley and from Oxdon to Triumph twice, and all other road sections once. There are many such routes each of length 125 miles. It is assumed the favourite restaurant is at the end of the shortest route, Kawaport.

The solution to the puzzle relies on making the network traversable. As it stands it contains six odd nodes, namely, those at Suziwich, Harley, Yamapool, Oxdon, Triumph, and Kawaport. To make it traversable it is necessary to convert it to a network with just two odd nodes by repeating two of the road sections linking odd nodes. The most efficient way of doing this has already been given.

52 Count the spots

Each of the seven numbers occurs eight times. Once with itself, and once with each of the other six numbers. It follows that there are 28 dominoes, and
$8(1 + 2 + 3 + 4 + 5 + 6) = 168$ spots.

53 Magic windmills

Let the magic total be T then

$$(a + b + c) + (d + c + e) + (f + e + g) + (b + f + h) = 4T$$

but

$$a + b + c + d + e + f + g + h = 36$$

so
$$b + c + e + f + 36 = 4T$$

now
$$1 + 2 + 3 + 4 \leqslant b + c + e + f \leqslant 5 + 6 + 7 + 8$$
$$\Rightarrow \quad 10 \leqslant b + c + e + f \leqslant 26$$
$$\Rightarrow 36 + 10 \leqslant 4T \leqslant 36 + 26$$
$$\Rightarrow \quad 12 \leqslant T \leqslant 15$$

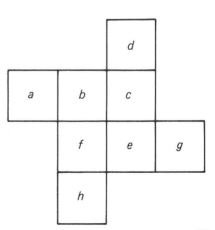

A solution for each possible total is shown, but others are possible. To find a solution, take a value for T, say 14, then $b + c + e + f = 4T - 36 = 20$. But $(a + b + c) + (f + e + g) = 2T$, so it follows that $a + g = 28 - 20 = 8$. Similarly $d + h = 8$. A solution can now easily be found..

87

```
      7                     7                   2                    2
 4  6  2              2  6  5             3  7  4              1  8  6
    1  3  8              4  1  8             1  8  5              3  7  5
    5                   3                   6                    4
```

54 Only six straight lines

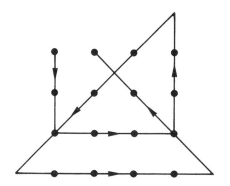

55 Correct these sums

(a) Unique solution $138 \times 138 = 19044$

(b)

85411	84011	74611
85411	84011	74611
0394	3590	2096
171216	171612	151318

56 Railway rotations

As only one station is empty at a time, the train movements are determined by which train moves into the empty space. One solution is given by

G F C G F A B D A C H A C B D C B

but you may find one requiring fewer moves.

57 Back in line!

Move each of the tail-up coins in the first column or the first row to the other end of their rows or columns, and use them to push these rows or columns one coin width to the left or down.

88

58 Remove a rectangle

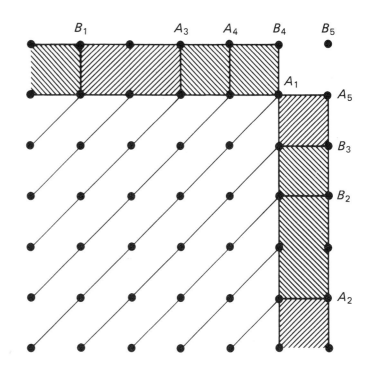

This game can easily be played on spotty paper or squared paper or, perhaps even better, on a geo-board using elastic bands.

The person who starts should win, but the strategy is not at all obvious unless the starting array is a square. In this case the starting player should choose the diagonal point nearest the top right-hand corner and then mirror every move his or her opponent makes. A win is assured as a study of the diagram below will indicate. Again *A* moves first.

59 Measuring the diagonal of a brick

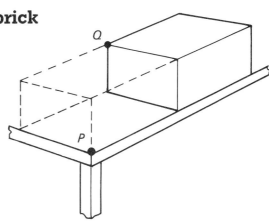

Place the brick at the corner of a table then move it along one edge equal to its length. The length of the diagonal is then easily measured, as shown in the diagram, from the corner of the table at *P* to the corner of the brick at *Q*.

60 Domino knots

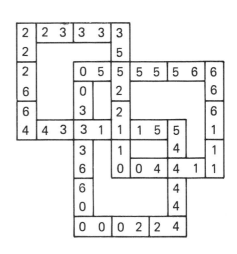

89

61 Jinxed!

She lived on the sixteenth floor.

Suppose, on average, with stops, the lift takes 15 seconds per floor, then it will take 10 minutes to make a complete cycle, of which 8 minutes would be spent below the sixteenth floor, and 2 minutes above. Hence when Leela arrives wanting a lift there is a 4 to 1 chance that it is on a lower floor, so will reach her travelling upwards.

63 The diabolical cyclone

The numbers on the spokes correspond to the numbers of the 4 × 4 magic square described by the notable Victorian puzzler H. E. Dudeney as the most magic, and which he called Diabolic or Nasik. These squares have the property that their semi-diagonals also total 34. There are 48 of these, so this puzzle has many solutions.

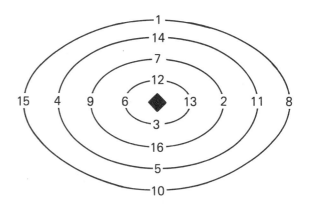

15	4	9	6
1	14	7	12
8	11	2	13
10	5	16	3

64 Two coin conundrums

The key to solving the second puzzle was to appreciate that coins could be stacked on top of each other. Then the triangular arrangement with two in the middle satisfies the requirements.

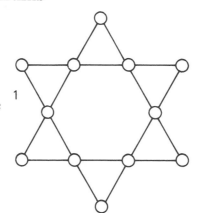

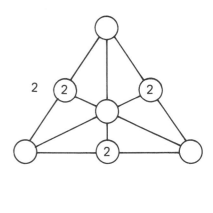

90

65   Triangular stamps

Two basic solutions to achieve 1 to 10, as shown. If the islanders were really imaginative they could manufacture their blocks of four stamps as tetrahedra, with the four faces having the values 1, 2, 4 and 8 cents. Then it would be possible to tear off blocks of stamps to any value from 1 to 15.

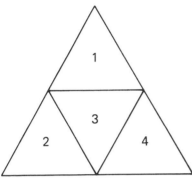
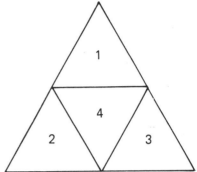

66   Decimated!

Order of boys and girls around the circle:

   BBGBBBGGGGGBBGGBBBBGBGGGBGGBBG

Counting in sevens would produce the best possible mix of boys (B) and girls (G), namely, 8B + 7G and 7B + 8G.

67   The vanishing act

Your eyes don't deceive you, there are only eleven lines after you have slid the paper along. However the lines have all grown slightly in length. The original total length of the twelve lines together was $12 \times 3 = 36$ cm.
The length of the new lines is 36 cm $\div$ 11 = $3\frac{3}{11}$ cm.

Measure with your ruler to see the increase in length. If you had started with 25 lines of length 3 cm, and say 1 cm apart, then this process would have led to 24 lines of length $3\frac{1}{8}$ cm.
Investigate.

68   Locate the primes

None of them are!
The digit sum, $1 + 2 + 3 + \ldots + 9 = 45$, and as 45 is divisible by 3, all such numbers have 3 as a factor so cannot be prime.

69 WARTS into STRAW!

The following solution using 26 moves may be the most efficient, but the author would be interested to hear from anyone finding a better one. The notation is: u = up, d = down, r = right, l = left.

A(urr), T(ddl), R(u), S(lld), W(rrrr), S(ull), T(uul), R(dd), A(ddr), R(u)

If you want a further challenge transform BLEAT to TABLE.

70 All present!

$11\ 826^2 = 139\ 854\ 276$	$19\ 377^2 = 375\ 468\ 129$
$12\ 543^2 = 157\ 326\ 849$	$19\ 629^2 = 385\ 297\ 641$
$15\ 681^2 = 245\ 893\ 761$	$23\ 178^2 = 537\ 219\ 684$
$18\ 072^2 = 326\ 597\ 184$	$29\ 034^2 = 842\ 973\ 156$

Squaring the number in your calculator will give the first six or seven digits correctly. Then squaring the last two or three digits will give the remaining digits of the product.

71 Catch your shadow

B always moves in a direction which is +90° to that of A and through twice the distance. A will only coincide with its image if it moves to the point C, see the diagram where

$$\angle ACB = 90° \text{ and}$$
$$BC = 2AC$$

Try programming this activity on your micro.

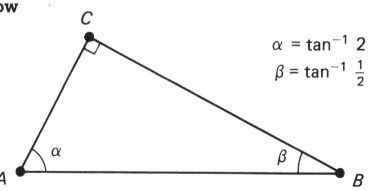

$$\alpha = \tan^{-1} 2$$
$$\beta = \tan^{-1} \tfrac{1}{2}$$

72 Prime magic

Although close in total to the one given, it has no prime in common. This puzzle was originally set by the author in the magazine *Teaching Mathematics and its Applications*, and readers might be interested in a more detailed discussion of the solutions in Vol. 3, No. 2 and No. 3, 1984.

83	89	41
29	71	113
101	53	59

73 Amoeboid patterns

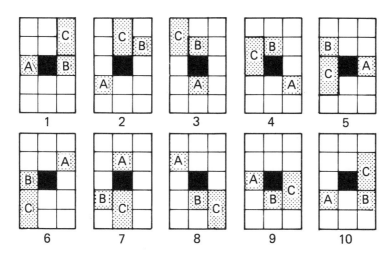

The amoeba is made up of four pieces: the centre square which is fixed, together with squares *A* and *B*, and domino *C*. The pattern is generated by *A*, *B* and *C* sliding anticlockwise around the fixed square, one square at a time, without turning. If, as at stage 3, domino *C* blocks the movement of *B*, then *B* stays put until the next move.

A little thought shows that square *A* would make one circuit around the fixed square in eight steps if unimpeded. But the domino will take ten moves to complete a circuit. At stage 3 and stage 8 as shown, *B* has been impeded so that *A* has almost caught up to it, and will do so at stage 13. From then on *A*, *B* and *C* remain in contact with one another and generate a recurring sequence of amoeboid shapes with a cycle of ten moves. But the first shape will never recur.

74 Waste not, want not!

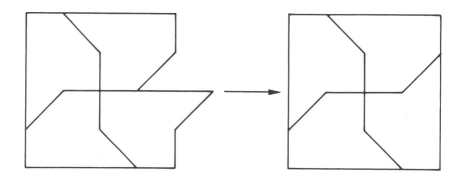

77 The starting grid

Al B5 C4 D3 E2
D4 E3 A2 Bl C5
B2 Cl D5 E4 A3
E5 A4 B3 C2 Dl
C3 D2 El A5 B4

78 Intersecting circles

A torus has the required
property.

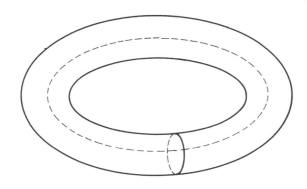

79 Can you help the block manufacturer?

The dimensions of the block, to the nearest tenth of a centimetre, will need to be

15.9 cm × 12.6 cm × 10.0 cm

To see this, suppose the block has dimensions

$a \times b \times c$ where $a > b > c$

then, after cutting, what was the end face of the original block will correspond to the top face in the half block whose shortest edge will be $a/2$. Thus

$a:b:c = b:c:a/2$

$$\Rightarrow \frac{a}{b} = \frac{b}{c} = \frac{2c}{a}$$

from which $ac = b^2$ and $ab = 2c^2$.

Eliminating a between these two equations gives

$b^3 = 2c^3$

Hence

$$\frac{b}{c} = \sqrt[3]{2} = \frac{a}{b}$$

so

$a:b:c = 2^{2/3}:2^{1/3}:1$

From this it is interesting to observe that all the rectangular faces of the original block (and half blocks) are the same shape with edges in the ratio $2^{1/3}:1$ which is approximately 1.26:1.

As the half blocks have the same shape as the original they too can be halved to produce blocks with the same shape, and so on.

80 The cyclo-cross race

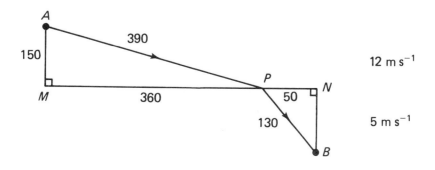

The diagram gives the optimum solution

$$t_{AB} = t_{AP} + t_{PB}$$

$$= \frac{390}{12} + \frac{130}{5} = 58.5 \text{ seconds}$$

This is probably best attempted by trial and error using a calculator or micro to do the arithmetic. The theoretical solution requires the result that for the fastest route

$$\frac{\sin \angle MAP}{\sin \angle NBP} = \frac{\text{speed in first medium}}{\text{speed in second medium}}$$

Justifying this is well within the scope of an A-level maths course, using calculus, but then the equation to give the actual position of P is a quartic.

81 The unusual jigsaw

This is the simplest dissection possible of a rectangle into squares of different size. Beginning in the 1930s much research has been done on such dissections and a very interesting account of this by one of the researchers, William Tutte, is to be found in *More Mathematical Puzzles and Diversions* by Martin Gardner.

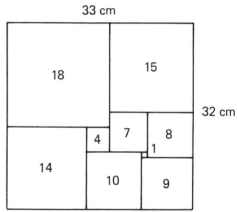

82 Palindromic termini

There are many 2-digit numbers with the given property. Any number *ab* where $a + b \le 9$ will always be a solution, for example

$$25 + 52 = 77, \qquad 32 + 23 = 55, \qquad 18 + 81 = 99$$

Further, any number *cd* where $c + d = 11$ leads to 121, for example

$$29 + 92 = 121, \qquad 47 + 74 = 121, \qquad 56 + 65 = 121$$

83 Star puzzle 2

The solutions shown were first found by Joe Gilks from Deakin University in Australia after the author posed the problem to delegates at a conference in Brunei in 1990. They are closely related to each other in that one solution can be obtained from the other by subtracting each of the entries from 13. In searching for the solution it is helpful to look at the possible distribution of odd and even numbers to give either odd or even totals. Simple algebra can also lead to the realisation that the total of the numbers in the points, and those in the interior, are divisible by 6.

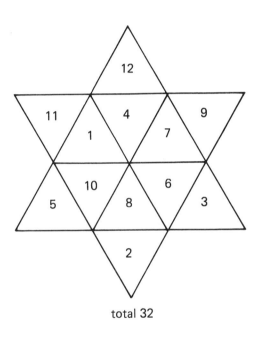

total 32

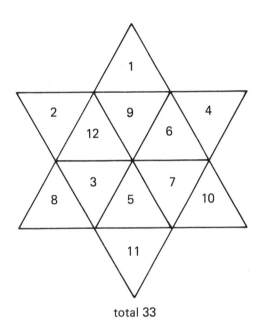

total 33

84 About turn!

The numbers will satisfy the 'about turn' condition if

$$ad \leqslant 9, \quad ae + bd \leqslant 9, \quad af + be + cd \leqslant 9,$$
$$bf + ce \leqslant 9, \quad cf \leqslant 9$$

Two solutions where no number is symmetric are:

$$312 \times 211 = 68952 \quad \text{and} \quad 213 \times 122 = 25986$$
$$123 \times 102 = 12546 \quad \text{and} \quad 321 \times 201 = 64521$$

```
        5 5 6 6 0 0
        5 5 6 6 0 0
    1 1 1 4 4 5 5 2 2 2
    1 1 1 4 4 5 5 2 2
        1 4 4 5 5 2
        0 0 2 2 3 3
        0 0 2 2 3 3
    3 3 3 6 6 1 1 4 4 4
    3 3 3 6 6 1 1 4 4
        3 6 6 1 1 4
```

```
2 2 4 4
2 2 4 4
3 3 5 5
3 3 5 5
```

(a)

```
    1 1 1 0 0 2 2 2
    1   1 0 0 2 2
        5 5 4 4
 6 6 6 5 5 4 4 3 3 3
 6 6 6 2 2 1 1 3 3
        2 2 1 1
        3 3 6 6
        3 3 6 6
 5 5 5 0 0 4 4 4
 5 5 5 0 0 4
```

```
2 2 4 4 1 1
2 2 4 4 1 1
3 3 5 5 0 0
3 3 5 5 0 0
```

(b)

```
 1 1 1 4 4 5 5 2 2 2
 1   1 4 4 5 5 2 2
     6 6 0 0 1 1
     6 6 0 0 1 1
     5 5 6 6 3 3
     5 5 6 6 3 3
 3 3 3 0 0 2 2 4 4 4
 3 3 3 0 0 2 2 4
```

```
        1 1 2 2
 6 6 6 1 1 2 2 5 3 3
 6 6 6 5 5 4 4 3 3
        5 5 4 4
```

(c)

On the face of it (c) might look the simplest, but note the lack of symmetry in the placement of the dominoes in the solution. In a set of dominoes every number occurs eight times so all these quadrilles contain two squares of each number. An example of a square and a rectangle are shown.

86 Subtraction to addition

The reason the method works becomes clear from the following:

$$573 - 489 = 573 + (1000 - 1000) - 489$$
$$= 573 + (999 + 1 - 1000) - 489$$
$$= 573 + (999 - 489) + 1 - 1000$$

The method is analogous to that used by computers to carry out subtraction, but there the numbers are stored in binary form. Thus instead of subtracting from a string of '9's, a string of '1's is used.

This operation is remarkably easy to perform as its effect is to change a '1' to a '0', and a '0' to a '1'. For example, $1111 - 1011 = 0100$.

Thus to find the result of $1100 - 1011$

$$\begin{array}{cc} 1100 \\ -\ 1011 \\ \hline \end{array} \quad \text{first} \quad \begin{array}{cc} 1111 \\ -\ 1011 \\ \hline 0100 \end{array} \quad \text{next} \quad \begin{array}{cc} 1100 \\ +\ 0100 \\ \hline 10000 \end{array}$$

and finally $10\,000 + 1 = 1$.

87 Start with any digit

(a) 239 and 4649 are the prime factors of 1 111 111 so

$$d \times 239 \times 4649 = d\ ddd\ ddd$$

and no other whole numbers would produce the same result, unless you accept 1 111 111 and 1.

(b) $73 \times 11 \times 101 \times 137 = 11\ 111\ 111$.

88 What route should the ant take?

Imagine half of the curved surface of the beaker flattened out into a rectangle, 8 cm × 9 cm. Reflect the position of C in the top edge of the rectangle. The shortest route for the ant is then given by $A \rightarrow B \rightarrow P \rightarrow C$. Now $BP + PC = BP + PC' = BC'$, but $BD = 8$ cm and $DC' = 15$ cm, so $BC' = \sqrt{8^2 + 15^2} = 17$ cm. Hence the shortest route is of length $25 + 17 = 42$ cm.

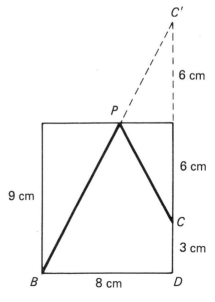

89   What were the stamps?

90   Vandalised!

The water level drops.

Iron is eight times heavier than water so when floating in the barge it displaces a volume of water equal to eight times its own volume. But when in the water it only displaces its own volume.

91   A calculator conundrum

The answer always appears to be a whole number. To see this is always the case note that

$$n(n + 1)(n + 2)(n + 3) + 1 = n^4 + 6n^3 + 11n^2 + 6n + 1$$
$$= (n^2 + 3n + 1)^2$$

92   The ship's masts

It is impossible to find the distance between the masts. The height at which the wires cross will always be 2.4 m no matter what the distance between the masts.

From the diagram, using similar triangles or enlargement

$$\frac{h}{4} = \frac{a}{a + b} \qquad\qquad (1)$$

$$\frac{h}{6} = \frac{b}{a + b} \qquad\qquad (2)$$

Dividing (1) by (2) gives

$$\frac{a}{b} = \frac{3}{2} \qquad\qquad (3)$$

Now from (1)

$$\frac{h}{4} = 1/(1 + \frac{b}{a}) = 1/(1 + \frac{2}{3}) \text{ using (3)}$$

$$\Rightarrow \frac{h}{4} = \frac{3}{5} \Rightarrow h = 2.4$$

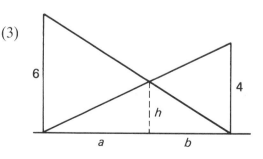

100

93 Help the book designer

24 cm high by 16 cm wide.
Find by trial and error or more directly by calculus.

If the height of the block of text is x cm its width will
be $216/x$, and the area of the page will be

$$A = (x + 6) (216 / x + 4)$$
$$= 4x + 240 + 1296/x$$

Differentiating and equating to zero for the turning points
leads to $4x^2 = 1296$, from which $x = 18$.

94 Orienteering

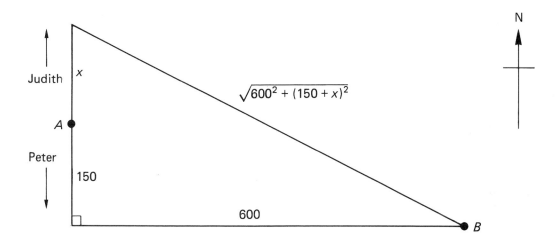

Assuming the ground they ran over was level, Ada ran
100 metres north. Using Pythagoras' theorem

$$150 + 600 = x + \sqrt{600^2 + (150 + x)^2}$$
$$\Rightarrow \qquad (750 - x)^2 = 600^2 + (150 + x)^2$$
$$\Rightarrow \quad 750^2 - 600^2 - 150^2 = 300x + 1500x$$
$$\Rightarrow \qquad\qquad 180\,000 = 1800x$$
$$\Rightarrow \qquad\qquad\qquad x = 100$$

95 · The circular square balance

One way of deducing the solution is as follows:

from $\qquad 2^2 + 49^2 = 14^2 + 47^2$
we get $\quad 49^2 - 47^2 = 14^2 - 2^2 = 192$

so it follows that if a and b are opposite numbers then

$$a^2 - b^2 = 192 \qquad (a + b)(a - b) = 192$$

Now

$$192 = 96 \times 2 = 48 \times 4 = 32 \times 6 = 24 \times 8 = 16 \times 12$$

Only even factors need be considered, for odd factors do not lead to whole number solutions for a and b. Taking $a + b = 96$ and $a - b = 2$ leads to $a = 49$ and $b = 47$ which were given, but

$a + b = 48$ and $a - b = 4$ gives $a = 26$ and $b = 22$
$a + b = 32$ and $a - b = 6$ gives $a = 19$ and $b = 13$
$a + b = 24$ and $a - b = 8$ gives $a = 16$ and $b = 8$
$a + b = 16$ and $a - b = 12$ gives $a = 14$ and $b = 2$

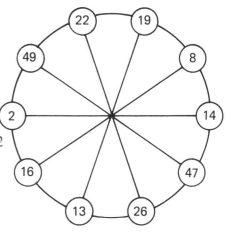

96 The cranky calculator

The solution depends on the identity

$$(x + y)^2 = x^2 + 2xy + y^2$$

From this

$$2xy = (x + y)^2 - x^2 - y^2 \qquad (1)$$

and xy could then be found by mental arithmetic.

However the calculator could be used to halve a given number X by using the identity

$$(X + \tfrac{1}{4})^2 = X^2 + \tfrac{1}{2}X + (\tfrac{1}{4})^2$$

for from this

$$\tfrac{1}{2}X = (X + \tfrac{1}{4})^2 - X^2 - (\tfrac{1}{4})^2 \qquad (2)$$

Thus given two numbers x and y the identity (1) can be used to find $2xy$ and then identity (2) to deduce xy.

97 Two squares to one

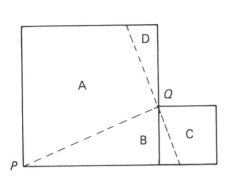

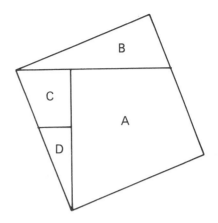

One solution is shown, but many pairs of lines drawn at the same angles to the squares would do. As drawn, *PQ* is the hypotenuse of a right-angled triangle whose sides are equal to the two given squares, so by Pythagoras' theorem *PQ* will be the required length for the single square with area equal to the sum of the two given.

By suitably positioning the line pair it is possible to cut the original squares into only three pieces and obtain a solution to the problem of forming a single square. How?

98 Self motivated!

Judy cycles 12 miles, leaves the cycle and jogs the remaining 9 miles. Nigel jogs 12 miles, then picks up the cycle and rides the remaining 9 miles. They each take 2 hours and 15 minutes.

99 Satisfying the Sultan's wives!

The first wife's problem is to place the flagpole to maximise the area of the smallest triangle. The best she can do is to place it on the line of symmetry to divide it in the ratio 3:1 making the two smallest triangles of equal area (37.5 km^2), and the two largest triangles of area 62.5 km^2. Clearly the Sultan favoured his second and third wives.

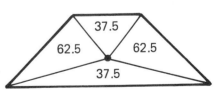

You may well have searched for a point where all the triangles are of equal area, but no such point exists.

This puzzle grew out of research carried out by the author and Professor R. B. Eggleton of Universiti Brunei Darussalam.

100 Complete the tetrahedron

Two possible answers. Either the tetrahedron has identical isosceles triangular faces with sides 5, 5, 6 or sides of 6, 6, 5. So the other four edges are of lengths 5, 5, 5 and 6, or 6, 6, 6 and 5.

101 Help the bosun

Using the notation of u, d, l, r for unit moves in the directions up, down, left and right, where the hold is seen as a 5 × 4 rectangle, a solution is as follows:

Fru, Eu, Hl, Id, Jd, Dr, Gu, Fl, Jl, Iu, Hr, Ed, Fd, Gd, Dl, Iu, Hul, Idd, Jru, Grr, Fu, Hu, Eu, Crr, Ad, Fl, Hl, Gl, Jdl, Iuu, Er, Cr, Ar, Fdd, Hld, Gll, Au, Cll, Ed, Id, Dr, Br, Gr, Hr, Fr, Cl, El, Id, Jr, Ar, Fru, Cu, Ell, Ad, Fr, Hr, Gd, Bl, Dl, Ju, Frr, Au, Err, Cd, Gd, Hd, Bd, Dll, Au, Hrr, Grr, Cu, Ell, Hdl, Il, Fdd, Jdd, Ar, Guu, Huu, Il, Jld, Ad.

102 Only 'takes' and 'adds'

Here are the eighteen solutions found by the author. Have you found any others?

$$98 + 7 + 6 - 5 - 4 - 3 + 2 - 1$$
$$98 + 7 - 6 + 5 - 4 + 3 - 2 - 1$$
$$98 + 7 - 6 + 5 - 4 - 3 + 2 + 1$$
$$98 + 7 - 6 - 5 + 4 + 3 - 2 + 1$$
$$98 - 7 + 6 + 5 + 4 - 3 - 2 - 1$$
$$98 - 7 + 6 + 5 - 4 + 3 - 2 + 1$$
$$98 - 7 + 6 - 5 + 4 + 3 + 2 - 1$$
$$98 - 7 - 6 + 5 + 4 + 3 + 2 + 1$$
$$98 - 7 - 6 - 5 - 4 + 3 + 21$$
$$98 - 76 + 54 + 3 + 21 \quad \text{(only four signs)}$$
$$9 + 8 + 76 + 5 + 4 - 3 + 2 - 1$$
$$9 + 8 + 76 + 5 - 4 + 3 + 2 + 1$$
$$9 - 8 + 76 - 5 + 4 + 3 + 21$$
$$9 - 8 + 76 + 54 - 32 + 1$$
$$9 - 8 + 7 + 65 - 4 + 32 - 1$$
$$-9 + 8 + 7 + 65 - 4 + 32 + 1$$
$$-9 + 8 + 76 + 5 - 4 + 3 + 21$$
$$-9 - 8 + 76 - 5 + 43 + 2 + 1$$

104   Calculator contortions

There are three main stages required to be able to find *xy*.

Stage 1
Square a given number by the following process:

$$\frac{1}{x} - \frac{1}{x+1} = \frac{1}{x^2 + x}$$

reciprocate to give
$$x^2 + x$$
take away *x* to give x^2

Stage 2
Use this ability to square a number to form 2*xy* from

$$(x + y)^2 - x^2 - y^2 = 2xy$$

Stage 3
Use the reciprocal function to extract *xy*:

$$\frac{1}{2xy} + \frac{1}{2xy} = \frac{1}{xy} \quad \text{reciprocate to give } xy$$

You may well decide that if Betty Bolzano was clever enough to deduce the above she would have found long multiplication just as fast as all the key pressing this method requires!
  Division could also be achieved as $x \times 1 / y$.

105   The magician's ribbon factory

There are many possible solutions, but two simple ones to make to baffle your friends are as follows:
(a) Use a cotton reel stuck on a dowel of a third its diameter, and wind separate pieces of ribbon on the reel and dowel. Then arrange that the dowel turns freely about a fixed axis in the centre of the box.
(b) Use two paper clips as the basis of a simple pulley mechanism. It is so light that, in the author's experience, it baffles and intrigues everyone. See the diagram.

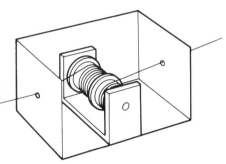

106 Domino Latin squares

None are possible!

If n is odd then n^2 is odd so such a square cannot be formed by dominoes. If $n = 2$ the only domino available for use in a Latin square would be 1–2. If $n = 4$ the only available dominoes are 1–2, 1–3, 1–4, 2–3, 2–4, and 3–4, and as there are only six of these they could not cover the sixteen squares required. A similar argument applies for the 6 × 6 square where only fifteen of the dominoes are appropriate.

107 Star puzzle 3

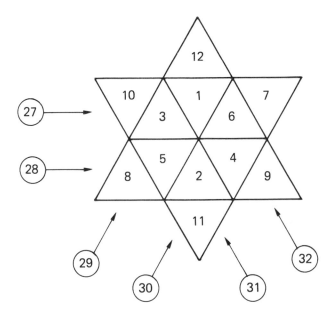

108 The medieval courtyard

The sides of the courtyard are approx 56.54 m. An easy problem to understand but not so easy to solve.

Let x and y be the distances of the well from two of the sides of the courtyard (see the diagram), then using Pythagoras' theorem:

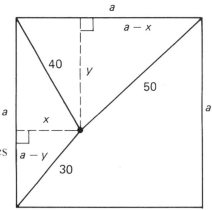

$$x^2 + (a - y)^2 = 900 \qquad (1)$$
$$(a - x)^2 + y^2 = 2500 \qquad (2)$$
$$x^2 + y^2 = 1600 \qquad (3)$$

(1) − (3) gives $a^2 - 2ay + 700 = 0$ (4)
(2) − (3) gives $a^2 - 2ax - 900 = 0$ (5)

Substituting from (4) and (5) for y and x into (3) gives

$$a^4 - 3400a^2 + 650\,000 = 0$$

which can be solved as a quadratic in a^2.

109 A Russian two-step

The method works because the halving process and selection of the odd numbers is essentially the process of converting the first number to a binary form. With the example discussed the remainders which are left at each stage are 1, 1, 1, 0, 0, 1 in that order from the top. Now

$$39 = 2^5 + 0 \times 2^4 + 0 \times 2^3 + 1 \times 2^2 + 1 \times 2^1 + 1$$
$$= 100111 \text{ in binary notation}$$

Thus 39_2 is formed by taking the remainders in reverse order.

$$39 \times 79 = (2^5 \times 79) + (2^2 \times 79) + (2 \times 79) + (1 \times 79)$$
$$= 2528 + 316 + 158 + 79$$
$$= \text{the sum of the numbers produced in the right hand column by the doubling process.}$$

110 Crossed ladders

This is an old chestnut which is not nearly as easy as it looks.
Using Pythagoras' theorem

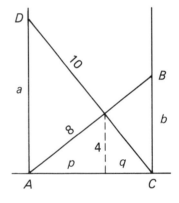

$$AC^2 = 10^2 - a^2 = 8^2 - b^2$$

so $a^2 - b^2 = 36$ (1)

Using similar triangles

$$\frac{4}{a} = \frac{q}{p + q} \qquad \frac{4}{b} = \frac{p}{p + q}$$

so $\dfrac{4}{a} + \dfrac{4}{b} = 1$ (2)

Rearranging (2) gives

$$b = \frac{4a}{a - 4}$$

and substituting in (1) gives

$$a^2 - \left(\frac{4a}{a - 4}\right)^2 = 36$$

which leads to the quartic equation

$$a^4 - 8a^3 - 36a^2 + 288a - 576 = 0$$

Solution by trial and error or more sophisticated numerical techniques leads to

$$9.25 < a < 9.255$$

from which $AC \doteqdot 3.8$ m

A similar problem which is easy to state but even harder to solve is that of finding the length of the tether of a goat attached to a ring at the edge of a circular field so that the goat has access to only half the field!

111   Political planning

The minimum total distance is achieved by taking the route:
Birmingham – Derby – Macclesfield – Stoke-on-Trent – Chester – Liverpool – Manchester – Leeds – Doncaster – Hull – Scunthorpe – Nottingham – Leicester – Birmingham.

112   The prime gaps

There are no primes between:
    1129 and 1151, 1327 and 1361, 1637 and 1657,
    1669 and 1693, 1951 and 1973.
It is easy to see that a sequence of composite numbers, (numbers not prime), can exist of any length. Suppose we want to show that such a sequence exists of length 100. Consider the sequence

    $101! + 2, 101! + 3, 101! + 4, \ldots, 101! + 100, 101! + 101.$

The number of the form $101! + n$ has n as a factor for all values of n from 2 to 101 inclusive. So none of the above 100 consecutive numbers is prime. This method can clearly be generalised.

113   Birthday products

The dates after Mary's fifteenth birthday when the special relationship holds are:

31/3/93	14/7/98
23/4/92	12/8/96
24/4/96	11/9/99
19/5/95	9/11/99
16/6/96	8/12/96

so the brothers' fifteenth birthdays must be on 23 April 1992, and 24 April 1996. Thus Mary was born on 13 July 1976, and her brothers on 23 April 1977, and 24 April 1981.

114   Dante's division

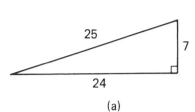

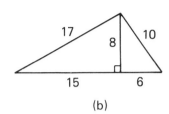

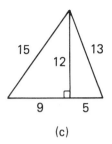

(a)   (b)   (c)

The triangles had sides as follows:
(i) 7 24 25 (ii) 10 17 21 (iii) 13 14 15
and the diagrams show how they can be found from
right-angled triangles.

Dante drew the third triangle, giving them the following
inheritances:

30 billion   28 billion   26 billion.

115   How long was the sermon?

$N = 34$.

Number of words

$= N.1 + (N - 1).2 + (N - 2).3 + \ldots + 2(N - 1) + 1.N$

$= \sum_{r=1}^{N} (N + 1 - r)r$

$= (N + 1) \sum_{r=1}^{N} r - \sum_{r=1}^{N} r^2$

$= (N + 1) \tfrac{1}{2}N(N + 1) - N(N + 1)(2N + 1)/6$
$= N(N + 1) (3N + 3 - 2N - 1)/6$
$= N(N + 1) (N + 2)/6$

Taking one word to be equivalent to 1 second, a quick
search with the aid of a calculator shows that $N = 34$ gives
a sermon of length 1 hr 59 min, and by far the closest to
2 hr.

116 The square touch

It is possible. Imagine rotating the pairs of lines l_1, l_2 and m_1, m_2 about S so that they remain parallel, at right angles, and touching S. After rotating through 90° anticlockwise the pairs of lines will have changed places with each other. As the distance between m_1 and m_2 was initially greater than the distance between l_1 and l_2, then as they change places there must have been some angle when the distance between the parallel lines became equal.

This argument holds for any simple closed curve.

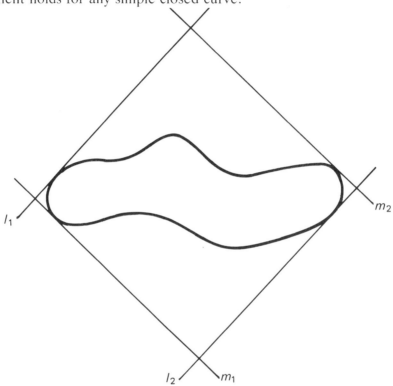

118 A cautionary tale

This is an example of what mathematicians call *ill-conditioned equations*. As given, the solution of the equation is

$$x = 1776 \qquad y = -4186,$$

but as given in the textbook the solution would be

$$x = -770 \qquad y = 1816.$$

Thought of as equations of straight lines it will be seen that their gradients are very nearly equal: -2.3585 and -2.3581 to 4 d.p. thus the slightest change of the gradient of one line radically changes the point of intersection of the two lines.

119 The wine importer

The consignment was 15 621 bottles.
The number of bottles left at the end of each day is

day 1 15 621 − 1   = 15 620
day 2 15 620 × 4/5 − 1 = 12 495
day 3 12 495 × 4/5 − 1 = 9995
day 4 9995 × 4/5 − 1   = 7995
day 5 7995 × 4/5 − 1   = 6395
day 6 6395 × 4/5 − 1   = 5115
day 7 5115 × 4/5 − 1   = 4092

which leaves him starting the eighth day with 4092 which
is not divisible by 5.

Let N be the initial consignment, and a_i the number of
bottles sold on the ith day after the consignment arrives
then:

$$N - 1 = 5a_1 \Rightarrow N + 4 = 5(a_1 + 1) \qquad (1)$$
$$4a_1 - 1 = 5a_2 \Rightarrow 4(a_1 + 1) = 5(a_2 + 1) \qquad (2)$$
$$4a_2 - 1 = 5a_3 \Rightarrow 4(a_2 + 1) = 5(a_3 + 1) \qquad (3)$$
$$4a_3 - 1 = 5a_4 \Rightarrow 4(a_3 + 1) = 5(a_4 + 1) \qquad (4)$$
$$4a_4 - 1 = 5a_5 \Rightarrow 4(a_4 + 1) = 5(a_5 + 1) \qquad (5)$$
$$4a_5 - 1 = 5a_6 \Rightarrow 4(a_5 + 1) = 5(a_6 + 1) \qquad (6)$$

Multiplying these six equations together and cancelling
common factors gives

$$4^5(N + 4) = 5^6(a_6 + 1)$$

Hence $N + 4$ is a multiple of 5^6, and the smallest value of
N for which this is true is $5^6 - 4 = 15\ 621$.

120 Area equals perimeter

This property is not as unusual as it first seems.
Suppose a rectangle has sides of length x and kx, where
$k > 1$. Then its area is kx^2 and its perimeter is $2x + 2kx$,
so for them to be equal

$$kx^2 = 2x + 2kx$$

from which

$$x = 2/k + 2$$

This equation gives a unique value for x for each
positive value for k, showing that there is a unique
rectangle with the given property once we know the ratio
of its sides.

For example, when $k = 2$ then $x = 3$ giving a 6 × 3
rectangle whose perimeter and area are both 18.

111

In general, given *any shape*, there will be one size for which its area will equal its perimeter. This is because changing the size of a shape by a linear scale factor of k will change the perimeter by a factor k but the area by a factor k^2.

121 Fix the watch towers

To find the minimum distance $PQ + QR + RP$ it is necessary to fix P, Q and R so that PQ and RQ make equal angles with AC, QR and PR make equal angles with AB, and RP and QP make equal angles with BC, as if the sides of $\triangle PQR$ are reflected off the sides of $\triangle ABC$. The points where this happens are at the feet of the altitudes of ABC, and the triangle formed by these points is known as the Schwarz triangle after the mathematician who first recognised its significance. The reflective nature of this triangle can be justified making use of elementary geometry, in particular the theorems involving circles (why is $AQPB$ a cyclic quadrilateral?).

The lengths of the sides of $\triangle ABC$ were carefully chosen so that P, Q and R fall at integral lengths along the sides as shown in the diagram.

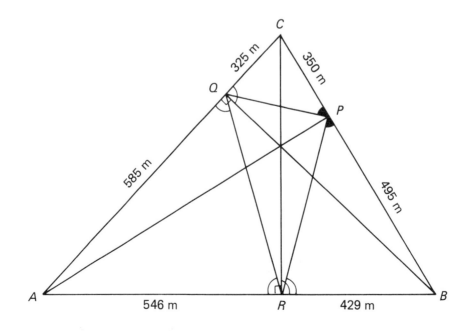

122 Truncating primes

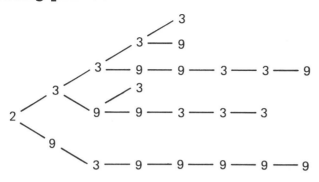

A table of primes and/or a computer program for testing which numbers are prime will speed this investigation along. The use of tree diagrams like the one shown is also very helpful. Even digits cannot occur apart from 2 at the start, and then the following digits can only be 3s or 9s as a 1 or 7 will make the number divisible by 3, and a 5 would make the number divisible by 5. The complete tree for the primes starting with 2 is given and shows there are 24 such primes.

The remaining such primes are summarised by giving the number corresponding to the end of the branch of its tree diagram.

31 193, 31 379, 317, 37 337 999, 373 393, 37 397, 3793, 3797, 53, 59 393 339, 593 993, 599.
719 333, 7331, 73 331, 73 939 133, 7 393 931, 7 393 933, 739 397, 739 399, 797.

123 Robotic rovings

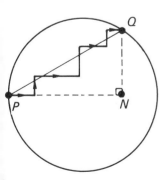 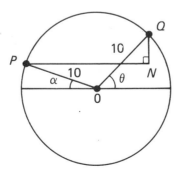 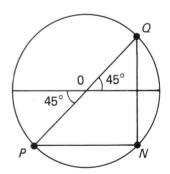

Clearly the longest route will start from the boundary at some point and end at a point on the boundary. The length of the route from P to Q is equal to $PN + NQ$. See the figure. Suppose OP is at an angle of α to the horizontal diameter, and OQ at an angle of θ as shown, where $\theta > \alpha$. Then the length of any path starting at P and finishing at Q is given by

$$L(\theta) = PN + NQ = 10 \cos \alpha + 10 \cos \theta + 10 \sin \theta - 10 \sin \alpha$$
$$\text{and} \quad L'(\theta) = 10 \, (-\sin \theta + \cos \theta)$$

which is zero, and the condition for a maximum, when $\tan \theta = 1$. It follows that for $-135° \leqslant \alpha \leqslant 45°$ the longest route is achieved by finishing at Q where $\theta = 45°$. Further consideration shows that the longest route when:

(a) $45° < \alpha < 90°$ is achieved by having Q at the same level as P,
(b) $-180° < \alpha < -135°$ is achieved by having Q immediately above P,
(c) $90° < \alpha < 180°$ is zero.

Hence the optimum route is when $\alpha = -45°$ and $\theta = 45°$ giving $\max(PN + NQ) = 20\sqrt{2}$ m.

124 Climbing Mt Igneous

As the surface of the cone slopes at $60°$, the distance from the base to the vertex V is 2 km. If the curved surface is developed by imagining a cut from V to C, the point on the base midway between A and B, then a semi-circle results whose radius is 2 km, as the length of the curve $CABC'$ must be equal to the circumference of the base of the cone, 2 km. See the figure. The shortest route from A to B is then represented by the straight line ANB on the semi-circle, of length $2\sqrt{2}$ km. In practice this means that the shortest route from A to B loops up over the curved surface of the volcano as shown. Similarly the shortest route consistent with reaching the edge of the crater is represented by the line segments $AP + PB$ of length $2\sqrt{AN^2 + PN^2} = 2\sqrt{5 - 2\sqrt{2}}$ km. This will consist of two curved paths on the volcano's surface.

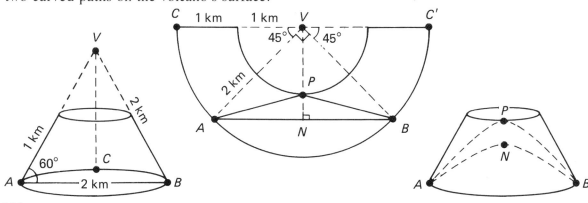

125 Round and around

This makes for an interesting investigation at a variety of levels, for at the basic level it only requires the ability to divide by a single digit, but the patterns which arise lead to a variety of hypotheses which can be tested.

4|102 564	4|923 076	4|307 692
025 641	230 769	076 923

4|820 512	4|512 820	4|205 128
205 128	128 205	051 282

When dividing by 2 the same cycle of 18 digits occurs no matter what the starting digit is

2\|526 315 789 473 684 210
263 157 894 736 842 105

2\|736 842 105 263 157 894
368 421 052 631 578 947

2\|947 368 421 052 631 578
473 684 210 526 315 789

To obtain a similar pattern when dividing by 3 a number based on a cycle of 28 digits is found to be needed:

└3 103 448 275 862 068 965 517 241 379┘

The lengths of these cycles and the sequence of digits may stir memories of recurring decimals (see *Mathematical Activities*, activity 128), and a few trials with your calculator will show that the cycles associated with 2, 3 and 4 are in fact the same as those found when dividing by 19, by 29 and by 39 respectively. But how can we make the connection between them?

Consider   4\|102 564
025 641

If instead of stopping after one cycle the process is continued and a decimal point is put after the 1, the division becomes

4\|1.025 641 025 641 025 641 025 64 . . .
0.256 410 256 410 256 410 256 41 . . .

Let

$$x = 0.025\ 641\ 025\ 641\ldots$$

then the division is of the form

$$\frac{4\,|1 + x}{10x}$$

Hence

$$40x = 1 + x$$
$$\Rightarrow 39x = 1$$

$$\Rightarrow x = \frac{1}{39}$$

Clearly a similar argument can be applied to all the divisions considered thus showing the link with recurring decimal cycles.

126 Pythagorean triples

Let $a = m^2 - n^2$ $\quad b = 2mn$ $\quad c = m^2 + n^2$ where m and n are any two positive integers, and $m > n$, then a, b and c form a Pythagorean triple.

Interestingly though, no algebraic identities of this kind are needed to prove Miranda's conjecture.

n $\quad$ 0 1 2 3 4 5 6 7 8 9
n^2 $\quad$ 0 1 4 9 16 25 36 49 64 81

The mapping $n \to n^2$ clearly shows that the unit's digit of any square number must be 0, 1, 4, 5, 6, or 9. It cannot be 2, 3, 7 or 8.

Consider now the effect on the unit's digit of adding two square numbers, see the table. If they are to form a Pythagorean triple, then the digit sum cannot be 2, 3, 7 or 8, so these have been crossed out. A scrutiny of the numbers remaining shows that at least one of a^2, b^2 or $(a^2 + b^2)$ is a 0 or a 5 in every case indicating that at least one of a, b, or c is divisible by 5. Did you also know that at least one of a, b, and c is also divisible by 3, and abc by 60? But that's another story!

(+) b^2	a^2 0	1	4	5	6	9
0	0	1	4	5	6	9
1		~~2~~	5	6	~~7~~	0
4			~~8~~	9	0	~~3~~
5				0	1	4
6					~~2~~	5
9						~~8~~

127 Tape recorder teaser

In 30 minutes the take-up reel has made $30 \times 60 = 1800$ revs. There will be 1800 layers of tape on the reel when fully wound. The total thickness of tape on the reel at this stage is 1.5 cm, so the thickness of the tape is $1.5 \div 1800 = 1/1200$ cm.

Suppose the length of tape is L cm, then the area of the total edge of the tape is $L/1200$ cm^2. But this must be equal to the area between the circles of radius 2.5 cm and 1 cm.
Hence $L/1200 = (2.5 + 1)(2.5 - 1)$, from which $L \approx 200$ m.
After t minutes the take-up reel has turned through $60t$ revs. so its radius will be $(1 + t/20)$ cm. Hence the circumference of the take-up reel at this time is $2\pi(1 + t/20)$ cm and as it is turning at 1 rev. s^{-1} the tape is being wound on at $2\pi(1 + t/20)$ cms^{-1}. This equals 11 when $t \approx 15$ min.

128 Achilles and the tortoise

Suppose Achilles gives the tortoise a 100 m start, and that the speeds of Achilles and the tortoise are 10 ms^{-1} and 1 ms^{-1} respectively. Then in 10 seconds Achilles will have reached the point where the tortoise started from, by which time the tortoise will have moved on a further 10 m. It will take Achilles 1 second to reach this point, by which time the tortoise will have moved on 1 m. To get to this point Achilles will take 0.1 second, and the tortoise progressed 0.1 m, and so on. The gap between them shortens by a factor of 0.1 at each step but the process goes on *ad infinitum!*

But can the tortoise ever be caught? The answer lies in summing the increments of time it takes Achilles to cover all the successive gaps between himself and the tortoise:

$$(10 + 1 + 0.1 + 0.01 + 0.001 + 0.0001 + \ldots) \text{ seconds}$$

Although there are an infinite number of time increments to consider, their sum is $11.11111\ldots = 11\frac{1}{9}$ seconds, a finite number. It is this realisation that the sum of an infinite number of numbers can have a finite sum which explains the paradox.

129 Form your conclusion

Let the various types of animals mentioned in the statements be denoted by a single letter as follows:

h animals in this house
c cats
p animals suitable for pets
g animals that love to gaze at the moon
d animals I detest
a animals I avoid
v carnivorous animals
n animals that prowl at night
m killers of mice
t animals that talk to me
k kangaroos

The ten statements can now be expressed in symbolic form to highlight their logical structure as follows

1 $h \to c$
2 $g \to p$
3 $d \to a$ which is equivalent to $\sim a \to \sim d$
4 $v \to n$
5 $c \to m$
6 $t \to h$
7 $k \to \sim p$ which is equivalent to $p \to \sim k$
8 $m \to v$
9 $\sim t \to d$ which is equivalent to $\sim d \to t$
10 $n \to g$

where $p \to q$ stands for the relation 'if p then q', and $\sim p$ for 'not p'. Thus statement 9 becomes $\sim t \to d$ which stands for 'if animals do not talk to me then I detest them'.
The 10 statements now all link toegether in a chain of implications:

$$\sim a \to \sim d \to t \to h \to c \to m \to v \to n \to g \to p \to \sim k$$

hence $\sim a \to \sim k$

which is equivalent to

$$k \to a$$

which put into English simply says
    'I avoid kangaroos'.